WITH OPEN ARMS: RECEIVING CARE WITH GRACE & GRATITUDE

THOMAS A. DROEGE

WITH OPEN ARMS

Author: Thomas A. Droege

Content Editor: Dr. Dick Hardel

Editor: Carolyn Berge

Cover Design: Jennifer Leonardson, Oxyjen Design

Interior Design: Carolyn Berge

© 2005 The Youth & Family Institute

ISBN 1-889407-46-1

Published by The Youth & Family Institute, Bloomington, MN 55431.
All rights reserved. No part of this book may be reproduced by any
means without written permission of the publisher.
www.youthandfamilyinstitute.org

This book was printed in part with a gift
from Wheat Ridge Ministries, which spreads
the seeds of hope throughout the world and
connects faith, healing, and wellness.
www.wheatridge.org

Scripture quotations unless otherwise noted are from New Revised
Standard Version Bible, copyright © 1989 Division of Christian
Education of the National Council of the Churches of Christ in the
United States of America. Used by permission.

Printed in the United States of America.

DEDICATION

To Esther, my wife of 50 years, whose caring presence
during my illness has enabled me to receive care more
graciously than I have in the past.

ACKNOWLEDGEMENTS

I could not have completed this book without the support
and assistance of many people, too many to acknowledge
them all. Three deserve special mention. Dr. Richard
Hardel of The Youth & Family Institute recognized the
value of a book on care-receiving when I first sent him the
manuscript. Working at an office located in a nursing
home, he and his staff were aware that receiving care was
difficult for many of the residents. After careful reading of
the manuscript, Dr. Hardel provided invaluable suggestions
for revising the book in ways that would make it more
accessible. A second person deserving special mention is
Elizabeth Droege, my sister-in-law, who served as editor of
the manuscript. Her suggestions for change were invariably
on target, leading always to greater clarity and readability.
Finally, I want to acknowledge the support of John Harris
and Linda Whitton, who first challenged me to undertake
this project.

CONTENTS

INTRODUCTION

The Youth & Family Institute studies research as to what is happening to children, youth, and families in the United States. We interpret that data to Christian congregations to help them strengthen families to nurture faith, live well in Christ, and pass on the faith. Our institute is about faith, renewal of home and congregation, and wellness. This book is about practicing faith to live well in Christ from milestone to milestone.

In *With Open Arms,* Dr. Droege takes us, the readers, deeper into a theology of the cross. He challenges us to understand God as relational power, the Trinity as both communion and suffering love. Droege also challenges us to think of God as receiver as well as giver. In Jesus we have a model of receiving as well as giving care.

One of the theological and foundational statements of The Youth & Family Institute is: "Faith is formed by the Holy Spirit through personal, trusted relationship, often, but not always in our homes." Droege helps us think about faith developmentally. Tending the baptismal journey or journey of faith must be in all the milestones of life from cradle to the grave. It is a journey that is not always pleasant, but also difficult and painful.

This book helps us tackle the tough questions of life. I have always believed that the toughest questions come to a person when experiencing the transition from being a caregiver to a time when he or she can only be a care receiver. Most people are not prepared for that transition. Depending on the cause of the transition, few people are able to respond effectively.

The power of this book is not only in the strength of Dr. Droege's gift as a teacher of practical theology, but mainly in his witness of his own experience. Practical theology begins with a human situation that calls for Christian action. It raises the questions that Droege raises: "Who is God?" "Where is God in this?" "Who am I?" "Where am I in relation to God?" "How am I doing according to God's standards?" "How can I do it better so people see God?"

In Droege's powerful, personal story, you will see him battling with his tough questions of life: "When I can no longer give to others, do I have any purpose and meaning in life?" "Can I just let my family and friends love me and support me, when I cannot respond in like manner?" "How can I learn to accept God's love when I can only receive from others?" As Tom battled with cancer, he continued to battle with self-worth and learning to be a receiver of care. Preparing the manuscript took years because of Tom's battle with his cancer. There were months and months when he could not respond clearly. His faith, love, and courage helps all of us learn to make our burdens and altar.

At The Youth & Family Institute we talk about four key practices of faith in our homes to nurture faith, live well in Christ, and pass on faith: Caring Conversations, Devotions, Service, and Rituals and Traditions. This is about faith formation and development. As we practice our faith, we are strengthened for now and better prepared for then, i.e., the transition from a care giver to a care receiver.

Dr. Dick Hardel
Director of Vision & Creative Ministries
The Youth & Family Institute

PREFACE

"It is better to give than to receive," as the Scriptures tell us, and contrary to conventional wisdom, it is a whole lot easier. Giving is a virtue, and the more you give, the more others will regard you as a good person, even a saint. Receiving has negative connotations for most adults: dependence, "on the dole," indebted. Not so for small children. Destined by nature to be completely dependent on the giving of others, they delight in the goodness of receiving. In the course of their gradual journey toward independence, they are taught by parents, teachers, and clergy to honor giving, if not delight in the goodness of it. Receiving prior to independence is natural and good; receiving as an independent adult is an art to be learned.

This book is about the art of receiving, not simply as a social grace, but as a practice of faith. Its focus is mostly on how one receives voluntary care that is provided out of love and compassion without any expectation of pay or other reward. Such care can become a burden to both caregiver and care receiver if it results in a prolonged dependence.

As a pastor and a counselor, I became aware of and sensitive to the needs of such people. I did that well, I think, through attentive listening to the stories of people who shared their innermost experiences with me. Though focused on the issues of receiving care, I gave scant attention to how I received care and for the most part was rarely conscious of receiving it at all. I gave care and others received it. It was a happy arrangement, and I thrived in the role.

A happy arrangement, perhaps, but not healthy. I learned this lesson the hard way when I was diagnosed with multiple myeloma, an incurable bone marrow cancer. For the first time since childhood, I was more a recipient than a giver of care, and I was woefully ill-prepared for the transition.

The difficult transition from caregiver to care receiver came slowly and haltingly. I began to reflect on the difficulties I was facing and wondered if my experience was unique. I engaged others in conversations about receiving care and discovered that their experience was similar to mine. I did a literature search on the art of receiving care and was astounded to find that there was next to nothing about the topic. A broad search of titles in the extensive theological library at Emory University, using the word *care* as the search term, resulted in 1,310 references. One title after another on giving care: pastoral care, lay caregiving, caring for particular populations (AIDS patients, alcoholics, chronic illness, dying), but only one title that gave any hint of receiving care.

It was thus that the idea for this book was formed. My goal has been to share my story and the stories of others who have lived with prolonged dependence on the care of others. Supported by a theology of receiving care and practical ways to learn the art of receiving care, such a book has the potential to prepare people for the almost inevitable times when they will need to receive care under difficult circumstances. I pray that they will learn to receive it with grace and gratitude.

Thomas A. Droege

part one

LEARNING ABOUT RECEIVING CARE FROM STORIES, RESEARCH, AND THEOLOGICAL REFLECTION

chapter one

IT IS HARDER TO RECEIVE
THAN IT IS TO GIVE:
A PERSONAL ACCOUNT

The butterfly counts not months but moments,
and has time enough. —Tagore

My sister Susanna and her husband Walt escaped the cold and snow of Michigan every winter for a camping trip to Florida and the Keys. They would regularly stop to see my wife Esther and me in Atlanta on their way south. Just weeks before their visit in January 1998 I had officially retired from a second career at The Carter Center. Esther and I were looking forward to a relaxed visit and the chance to catch up on news about family and mutual friends. We had lived in the same town in northwest Indiana for over 25 years, where Walt and I had shared the challenges and joys of teaching theology at Valparaiso University. There were so many things we had shared over the years.

The pleasant prospect of a casual and relaxed visit vanished the same week, interestingly enough, that my replacement at

The Carter Center was selected. Irregular blood counts from a routine annual physical exam yielded a devastating diagnosis of multiple myeloma, an incurable bone marrow cancer. All treatment options for this disease are palliative. They are useful only when the threat of the disease is greater than the threat of the treatment.

Trained as an academic, I immediately plunged into the research literature, the most depressing reading I have ever done. There are major complications: bone deterioration leading to fractures and spinal compression, renal failure, a compromised immune system that can be overwhelmed by bacterial infection in a single day. At that time (January 1998) the median survival time was 30 months, though with improved therapies it is now three to five years. I was a basket case by the time our guests arrived in late January.

Susanna and Walt's visit could not have come at a better time. Though Esther and I have good friends in Atlanta and a wonderful congregation of caring people who would provide sustained support in the months and years ahead, it was literally a God-send for us to have my sister and her husband here that weekend. They met my need for unhurried and extended conversation about this horrible turn of events and what it might mean for our future.

I hated to see them go and was envious of their trip to the Keys. Both Esther and I needed some relief from the chill of winter and the dark cloud hovering over our lives. The sunshine and warmth of the Keys sounded very inviting.

Without making a big deal out of it, we told Susanna and Walt to let us know if they saw a rental sign or heard about a place that was available for a week. Not much hope of that-it was the peak season for northerners to seek the sand and sun of the south. In fact, Walt and Susanna were already making phone calls to reserve a camping site for the following year.

We were stunned a week later when we got a phone call from

them informing us that they had found a place, but not without considerable searching, as I found out later. It was a lovely new home in Marathon, halfway down the Keys, and located right on the waterfront. The rental came with exquisite furnishings. It was expensive, and I would immediately have said it was more than we could afford, but Susanna had already arranged with our other three siblings to pay most of the week's cost.

What that meant to me at the time is reflected in a report I sent to family upon our return:

> I can't begin to thank you enough for your contribution to this vacation. It's not so much the monetary gift (though that's greatly appreciated!), as it is the expression of solidarity with me as I come to terms with what lies ahead. What prompts that comment is one of my favorite folk songs about a man who goes through chemo, loses all his hair, and comes home from the hospital very self-conscious about his baldness. He opens the door to his house and is welcomed by a roomful of family and friends, all of whom had shaved their heads as an expression of their strong identification with his suffering. Now I'm not suggesting you go that far! What you did do, however, is very much like that for me, and I thank you from the bottom of my heart. It will always be one of the best memories of my life.

That week marked a major transition in my learning to cope with a disease that I would have to live with for the rest of my life. The devastation I felt before we went to the Keys was complete. I saw no light at the end of the tunnel, only darkness pressing in on every side with the prospect of a diminished and foreshortened life. It felt like a mist had settled over me and all my surroundings, and I had to grope to find my way.

During the week in the Keys, the mist gradually began to lift and, wonder of wonders, all the furniture was rearranged. It was nothing less than a transformation, not just of me but of the world I was living in. Nothing was the same any more, and as often happens in new surroundings, I had a heightened sensitivity to everything around me. I became more aware, more mindful, and more appreciative of every day, every hour, every moment, and more likely to celebrate life than ever before. Though the transformation was by no means complete by the end of this week, I was aware that a major shift in self-consciousness had occurred.

The wonderful gift of this week from my sisters and brothers also marked another major transition in my life: a beginning awareness that I could receive care without being embarrassed by it. For once in my life I received a generous expression of care without feeling like I needed to protest, to say they should not have done it, that I didn't deserve it. Nor have I ever felt in the least indebted. I was able to receive this gift graciously and with heartfelt gratitude.

I was aware already then of a shift in self-awareness that created a space for me to receive expressions of love and caring from others. It was just a beginning and did not alter my core identity as a giver of care. That's too deeply embedded in roles that have shaped the sense of who I am throughout my adult life—as husband, father, pastor, teacher, counselor, and chaplain. However, the foundations of my identity as a giver of care were shaken by the simultaneous occurrence of my retirement (no longer a professional caregiver) and my cancer diagnosis (now a patient receiving care). What emerged was a gradual shift away from an awareness of myself as a caregiver, making room for a new awareness of myself as a receiver of care. This new awareness was like the emergence of tender shoots from newly planted seeds. I am content to nurture this tender but growing awareness of myself as a receiver of care, receptive to all the love and prayers that others graciously shower upon me.

Perhaps I'm overstating the case. I know full well that I have been on the receiving end of care since the day I was born. For the first twenty years of my life I was dependent on the care of parents, older siblings, teachers, pastors, and extended family. Throughout my long career as a student I was dependent on the wisdom and guidance of instructors and mentors. Esther and I have been interdependent throughout our married life. Above all, I have believed for as long as I can remember in the gospel proclamation that all of life is a gift from God, dependent on God's gracious care.

Ten years ago I would freely have acknowledged everything I just said about receiving care, but I simply took all that for granted without paying much attention to it. My identity as a caregiver, however, has been carefully cultivated. Years of training and practice as a pastor, a chaplain, and a therapist have shaped that identity, along with the experience of parenting three daughters. It's no wonder that a gradual shift in self-awareness from a giver of care to a receiver of care has been difficult and sometimes jarring.

Receiving the perfect gift of a transformational week in the Keys when I needed it most made a deep impression on me. I decided to pay more attention to my needs and attempt to relearn the lost practice (and it takes practice!) of receiving care. It has not been easy. I continue to encounter enormous resistance from a deeply embedded sense of self-sufficiency. When someone asks me how I am (not "How's it goin'?" but "How are you, really?"), my first instinct is to say, "I'm fine. I'm managing just fine." It's only later that I'm fully aware of whether it was an honest answer. Sometimes it is. Sometimes it isn't. The point is that I have to be self-conscious about asking for help or responding to expressions of care, while giving care comes automatically when I sense needs in others.

The first big step in consciously practicing the art of receiving care came with the decision to share the story of my illness with anyone who was interested. Though I didn't want to be defined by the illness, I didn't want to be alone with it either. This was one of the best decisions I made in learning to cope with my illness. I sent an e-mail report to family and friends, and I continued that practice after each three-month check-up for three years. I encourage people to ask about my health and how I'm coping with this disease. As never before, I understand the oft-quoted statement of John Donne that "no man is an island," that all of us need a community of support and love to sustain us in time of need.

That fortuitous decision brought me a ton of support in the form of phone calls, promises of prayer, and e-mail responses of encouragement. People praised me for being open. I learned, however, that there's a big difference between receiving spontaneous expressions of love and support and accepting concrete offers of help. A whole new level of resistance emerges in me at that point. I cite but one of many possible examples:

Esther and I both snore. We often joked about it, but it was not a big problem for either of us until I began to sleep more lightly because of myeloma-related bone pain. More and more I found it difficult to get back to sleep. My solution was to leave the bedroom and sleep on a sofa the rest of the night. When I did that, Esther said I should wake her on such occasions and she would sleep elsewhere. I said, "I won't do that. This is my problem, not yours." She responded as I would have in her situation: "You're the one in pain. You should stay in your own bed." Then it suddenly dawned on me that I was being a lousy care receiver in refusing her gracious and loving offer of help. That happens more often than I'd like to admit.

I discovered yet another level of resistance when I needed to ask for help. Like most Americans, I value my independence and ability to solve problems on my own. Despite the exasperation of my wife, I'm rarely willing to pull off the road and ask for directions when I'm driving and can't find my way.

This is such a deeply ingrained trait that I honestly cannot remember a time after I left home that I asked for anything from my parents or siblings. It's not that I was never offered help; I just didn't ask for it. I had a good relationship with my parents and get along well with my four siblings. For the past two decades we and our spouses have spent a weekend together every fall. But until recently, we rarely talked to each other about our needs or our vulnerabilities, and other than that annual fall weekend, we didn't keep in touch on a regular basis. Occasional phone calls and visits, e-mail messages, a Christmas letter—that was about it.

The refreshing experience of receiving care and the awareness of how much resistance I have to accepting it, much less asking for it, prompted me to reflect more deeply on the dynamics of receiving care. I brought it up in conversations with others, asking about their experiences. The more I talked about it, the more stories I heard about others' difficulties in receiving care graciously.

I developed a questionnaire on receiving care for use in groups and workshops. (It is printed in Chapter 6 as part of the first workshop exercise.) The data I gleaned from these surveys gave me valuable feedback on how people generally dealt with this aspect of their experiences. Though far short of a scientific survey, what I found does permit some broad generalizations. I will draw on those findings in subsequent chapters.

One inescapable conclusion is that people have a hard time receiving care, especially when their need for care is prolonged and disproportionate to the care they give in return.

This is particularly true for self-conscious caregivers, both professionals and those heavily invested in caring for their children and, often, their parents. They generally ignore their own need to receive care, and have difficulty identifying with the experience of receiving on the part of those they are serving. This is true of even the most empathic caregivers because that aspect of the experience is so atrophied. It is for such people that this book is written.

It has been over six years since the fateful month of January 1998, when I retired and within two weeks was diagnosed with multiple myeloma. That's a long survival time for a myeloma patient, about twice the time I anticipated. Even more remarkable is that for five and a half years I received no treatment other than a monthly infusion for the protection of bones. Every three months an assessment of disease activity indicated no need to initiate therapy.

I've culled some excerpts from quarterly reports to family and friends that offer at least a glimpse into my growing awareness of the gift of health and the goodness of receiving much love and support from family and friends:

February 1998

I'm relieved to have the prospect of two more months free of symptoms from either the disease or the side effects of treatment. I measure time in months now and am deeply grateful for every symptom-free day. I've been grateful for excellent health throughout my life, but never as grateful as now. And I do feel healthy, with as much energy as I ever had.

November 1998

Why is my disease stable while others are struggling to survive with very aggressive forms of myeloma that can bring death within months? What part do faith and prayer play? There is no way to answer that by means of strict empirical evidence, though some scientific studies suggest that it is a significant factor. I firmly believe that your prayers and my spiritual practice are significant factors in my current health status. And I know that my spiritual health has been strengthened beyond measure by the experiences of the past year.

For all of us, life is a matter of sustained blessings, even in the midst of suffering-perhaps especially then. Close to the top of the list of my blessings are your prayers and support. Thank you!

June 1999

It's been almost a year and a half since my diagnosis and, thank God, there have been no symptoms, no toxic treatment, and little change in the status of the disease. In some ways it's a little embarrassing-so few external indicators to warrant all the prayers and support I've received. I can live with that embarrassment a lot longer, and I welcome your prayers and expressions of support.

August 1999

Beyond the spiritual growth I've experienced, the greatest blessing of these past months has been the care I've received from family and friends. I've been a giver of care most of my life but have rarely paid much attention to the receiving of it. That's changed, though I still feel awkward in the role. I think maybe all of us have a lot to learn about this, especially those of us who are male.

May 2000

It's been two years since my diagnosis. Based on survival statistics, one half of those diagnosed the same time as I was are now dead. Reflecting on that brings a flood of different emotions: survival guilt (why me and not others?), a deeper appreciation of the power of prayer and personal support, but above all an overwhelming sense of gratitude for the amazing grace of God. My spirituality has always been rooted in gratitude, but never more than now. Gratitude for every breath, each coming as a gift. Gratitude for this moment right now, this precious moment. Gratitude for hope that is rooted deep in promise—no matter how dark the shadows, how weak the body, how cloudy the mind, how dull the spirit. Thanks be to God!

January 2001

It's been over eight months since I've sent you a report about my life with multiple myeloma. As has often been the case in the three years that I've been sending quarterly reports, I debated with myself about continuing that practice. As this message indicates, I decided to do so at least for now. My justification is that you need to hear good news as well as bad from cancer patients. You need to know that cancer can be a chronic condition as well as a critical illness.

So rejoice with me in what some would call good fortune but what I choose to call God's blessing and healing. I appreciate your prayers and yearn for more. Please do not grow weary in sustaining me with that loving support. I'm back on a quarterly checkup schedule, so expect to hear from me in three months with a message that I hope will be much the same as this one, along with a reminder of the wonder and goodness of being alive each and every day.

April 2001

The myeloma remains stable, something like a sleeping dog (would you believe that I initially typed it "god"?). It feels more like a sleeping tiger, as the Freudian slip would indicate. The disease is not going away (and won't) but it's not progressing. That's all that any myeloma survivor prays for.

I write this at the beginning of the Triduum, the high holy days that lead to and flow from the Easter Vigil and its wondrous linking of death, resurrection, and baptism.

It's the sacred story of these three days that enables me to live both realistically and hopefully under the shadow of death that is never far from my consciousness.

November 2001

I write this on Thanksgiving and have no difficulty evoking a deep sense of gratitude to God and to all of you for your enduring support. I am saddened, however, when I think of all the illness and tragedy that has crept into the lives of good friends who were perfectly healthy when I was first diagnosed in January 1998. We hardly need to be reminded of our vulnerability these days. May that awareness deepen your sense of gratitude, as it has for me.

June 2002

Thank you for your support and prayers. There's no study to show what difference that makes, if any, in the survival of myeloma patients, but my intuition and faith tell me that the difference is huge. Whatever the difference for my physical well-being, I know I need your continued support and prayers for my spiritual well-being. I receive it with joy and gratitude.

For five and a half years I had no physical symptoms of disease activity, and thus was no more dependent on receiving physical care than I was before my diagnosis in 1998. That changed rather dramatically in mid-July of 2003 during my annual visit to John and Linda, best friends from Valparaiso, on Prince Edward Island in Canada. They had bicycles that rode close to the ground and had a different sense of balance because the front wheel was larger than the rear. After practicing near the house, Linda and I took a ride on a dirt road away from traffic. The front wheel of my bike climbed the edge of one of the ruts, and the bicycle came out from under me. I landed flat on my back. I sustained a compression fracture but no stenosis (closing between vertebrae) or spinal chord involvement. However, the muscle damage was severe and improved only in small increments in the months following.

Linda is one of the best caregivers I know. I've seen her in action numerous times, also in relation to me since the time of my diagnosis. The physical care she provided with moist hot packs, nourishing food, and assistance in getting medical advice was soothing to both body and spirit, and I was able to receive it without my usual resistance. The same was true of John, who has given me counsel and aid on many occasions, and was particularly helpful in preparing me for the dreaded trip from Canada back to Atlanta.

The quality of care continued when I got back to Atlanta. The need for care was even greater then because I began a rigorous six-month treatment protocol for myeloma that caused severe side effects. Esther, a nurse by training, had the good judgment to encourage me to do everything I could for myself, but she has always been ready to do for me what I can't manage. Our daughter, Karla, who is living with us while she pursues an acting career, has been a good conversation partner. She inquires almost daily about how I am, how I really am, and is willing to take as much time as necessary to hear the answer and respond appropriately. As with most people these days, but especially with Karla, I get beyond superficial answers and say honestly how I'm really feeling. That's been difficult for me to do in the past, but I do it now easily and without embarrassment.

The biggest breakthrough for me was the decision to purchase an expensive hot tub and have it installed adjacent to the deck in our backyard. This was a lesson in giving care to and receiving it from myself. I had thought about installing a spa for years, prompted by the encouragement of my son-in-law, who had installed one in his home. I resisted the idea for all the usual reasons—too much expense, sheer luxury, much better ways to use the money. This time was different. The need for the tub as therapy for a badly bruised back was evident, and I was much better now at receiving care, even from myself.

These examples mark a distinct transformation in my history of care-receiving. I wish I had been better prepared for receiving care before I assumed the role of care receiver, but my experience is testimony that you can make adjustments once you are thrust into that role if your health permits self-awareness and you have sufficient time.

I wish I could conclude this chapter by saying that after six years of living with an incurable cancer and literally thousands of expressions of love, support, and prayers, I can now receive care graciously and easily. Even if I were to receive the gift of yet another six years, I doubt that I would master the practice of receiving care. There is far too much personal and social investment in the myth of the heroic caregiver and the undeserving care receiver to overcome. Aware of my limitations, I will continue to seek an increased openness to receiving.

ADDENDUM
June 10, 2004—May 31, 2005

When I left for a family gathering in Crete in the summer of 2004, I had completed this manuscript, sent it to the publisher, and expected to do nothing more than edit copy prior to publication. However, a series of significant and life-threatening experiences after my return prompted me to ask for a publication delay so that I could incorporate what I had learned into the manuscript. I decided to keep the content of Chapter 1 in its original form and to add this Addendum. I have also revised the contents of the remaining chapters where appropriate to reflect these later insights.

The Experience of Transformation

The week after Esther and I returned from our glorious family reunion in Crete, I experienced severe digestive problems, which led to tests that revealed a parasite infection picked up while traveling overseas. In addition, myeloma lab tests indicated that my bone marrow cancer had become aggressive. The effect of this combined attack on my compromised immune system sent me on a four-month downward spiral that necessitated intensive hospital treatment.

While in the hospital, I experienced a shift in my identity as a child of God. The shift was both intense and dramatic. Like all experiences of this type, it is a struggle to find words to describe it, easier to say what it wasn't than what it was. It was not a new insight that suddenly came to me, as I have often experienced when wrestling with an issue that I had previously been unable to resolve. It was not a shift that occurred because of some decision I had made to alter my behavior in some way. Nor was it a shift that resulted from some insight about myself that came from the observation of someone else. I have had experiences like these that have been both intense and dramatic, and on rare occasions so intense that I felt like a different person.

The best word I can use to describe this experience is *transformation*. This experience of personal transformation was different from other experiences not just in degree, but in kind. What made it different was my seeming lack of involvement in the process. I was more observer than participant. It was a transformation that happened to me, and my experience came, as it were, after the fact. It's similar to what I've read in books describing near-death experiences. You are the same person as before, but you are an observer rather than a participant with respect to the event that triggers the experience.

The pattern, not the content, of the experience was similar to the conversion experiences described by William James in

Varieties of Religious Experience. The people he interviewed described a shift in the center of their consciousness, a shift from sin-sick souls to redeemed and forgiven children of God. Those he interviewed were consistent in describing their conversions as an act of grace, a gift from God to which they contributed nothing. Their identity in relation to God had shifted completely, and they spoke of the freedom and joy they experienced with this new status.

I did not have a conversion experience in the hospital, but rather a shift in the center of my consciousness that enabled me to experience my identity as a child of God in a deeper and more profound way than I had ever known before. As with those James interviewed, I had done nothing to bring this about. I remember feeling stunned, excited, and full of restless energy at this discovery.

Never do I recall feeling so overwhelmed by an experience, so sure that the transformation I felt came from God as pure gift. Never have I been so sure that nothing could separate me from the love of God in Christ, that my life was hidden with Christ in God. The experience was completely unexpected. Though critically ill at the time, I had no fear or dread of death prior to this experience. Thus it was not an answer to fervent prayer. It simply happened. I found myself in a different place, a more secure place. I was intensely aware of what I was seeing and feeling, more mindful than I had ever been during my daily meditation practice.

As I had done nothing to bring about this deeper awareness of who I was as a child of God, I knew that its continuation was in God's hands and that there was nothing I could or needed to do to maintain it. It was as if I could now watch my life as God's child unfold without any need or wish to control it. The most surprising part of this experience was the realization that I had put my life fully in God's hands, trusting completely in God's will. Yet it was not something I had done. I had not "surrendered" by trusting God's will rather than mine. I had done nothing, and that was the surprise. There was no exercise of discipline, no "practice" that enabled me to receive this gift.

Translating Experience into Insight for the Practice of Receiving Care

The challenge of incorporating new insights for the practice of receiving care after I had completed the manuscript was a more daunting task than I had anticipated. The intensity of the revelatory experience was so clear initially that I thought the revision of the manuscript would be relatively easy. I had not taken into consideration how severely the side effects from medication would restrict my capacity to write. The fatigue common among cancer patients receiving chemotherapy made it nearly impossible to stay alert and think clearly. As days and weeks passed with little written, the intensity of the experience faded, and I began to wonder if it was as significant as it had seemed at the time. Rather than the heightened experience of the presence of God that I had felt initially, the opposite seemed true. My meditation practice faded and then stopped completely. I was not able to remain alert and focused enough to maintain it. Fatigue and unremitting pain from peripheral neuropathy and my lower back crowded into my consciousness every waking moment. Despite my knowledge that God's loving presence was sure whether I experienced it or not, God never seemed more distant than in the dark days of the past three months.

Though I feel well enough at the moment to write, I am weary as I do so. I lack the mental energy that I usually have when I write. Does that invalidate what still seems a profound transformative experience as a child of God, even when I have to search for it in the fog of my brain? I don't think so, or I wouldn't continue to write. Perhaps the true test of any genuine expression of faith is not its vibrancy at the height of a revelatory experience, but its staying power when suffering squeezes out the vitality and leaves only the core of what one knows to be true at the deepest level of the self.

It's the experience that commands my attention as I reflect on the personal transformation I am describing. When I move from the experience to thought, to concepts that can capture the experience and convey it to others, I am on less sure ground. Language does not do justice to the experience. I make every effort to keep the language true to my experience, but it is at the same time removed from it in the way that all symbols are, even the metaphors and analogies that come closest to expressing the experience.

I draw heavily on Christian symbols to give meaning to the experience of my personal transformation. I do not think that my experience changes or adds to the Christian witness handed down through Scripture and tradition and which have always been the foundation of my faith.

However, I do recognize that I am in a unique position to draw out the implications in my experience for understanding the practice of receiving care and asking for help. That is my goal in the remaining portions of this book. Chapters 2 and 3 include sections that attempt to do exactly that.

I look to the openness of trees,
branches spread wide,
receiving.

And I wonder about the openness in me.

if my branches are tightly twined around myself
or reaching out.
receiving.

it is time I untwined what I can.
it is time I spread wide a heart much in need of
receiving.

chapter two

A THEOLOGY OF RECEIVING CARE

According to St. Paul, Jesus said, "It is more blessed to give than to receive" (Acts 20:35).

Gratitude has been at the heart of my spirituality for as long as I can remember, and increasingly so as I've created space and time over the past decade to be more attentive to my interior life. Somewhat surprisingly, my appreciation and gratitude to God for the goodness of life has increased exponentially since my diagnosis of cancer. The two are closely intertwined, because apart from the cancer diagnosis, I do not think I would have the same level of deepening awareness that everything I cherish, including my health, is like sand sifting through my fingers.

What I write about as a generalization in the above paragraph—my mindfulness and gratitude—moved to a new level six months ago. My purpose in this chapter, beyond providing a theology of receiving care, is to draw out the implications of the experience described in the addendum of Chapter 1.

What I now knew from experience, I had known theoretically most of my life: that I had little control over my health and the length of my life. Normally, loss triggers my frustration and anger, but instead I discovered an ever-deepening sense of gratitude. That might seem like evidence of denial, but it's not so surprising when you consider that from my earliest childhood I have been steeped in a theology of grace, which taught me that life is a gift, not a possession. It stands to reason that faith shaped by a theology of grace will see all of life as a gift of God, especially when life is threatened. Assurance of God's healing and comforting presence in my illness and my eventual death only deepens my sense of gratitude.

It is ironic that while I receive this gift from God with ease, there is so little carry-over between that and my relationship with others. If I can graciously, gratefully receive whatever flows freely from the loving hand of God, why is it so difficult for me to receive graciously from others, to ask for what I need, to nurture a spirit of receptivity?

The social dynamics that affect people's giving and receiving operate differently from the dynamics of faith in relation to God. It's almost as though I am two different people. I value God's loving care and nurture it through prayer, meditation, and worship. I resist care from others even when my need is great, relying instead on my own resources and even feeling superior to those who take more than they give.

Traditional Christian theology fosters this dual identity— receiver in relation to God and giver in relation to others. The heart of the gospel is that all is gift, that God is the source of all life and love. A Christian identity in relation to the gospel is that we are receivers, little more than beggars in relation to God.

At the same time we are to be like God the giver in relation to others. This calls for a radical shift in identity from receiver to giver. In a beautifully written book, *Altogether Gift,* Michael Downey describes the Trinity as God the Giver (Father), God the

Given (Son), and God the Gifting (Spirit). God is the source and ground of love, Christ the embodiment of God's love, and the Spirit the gifting of that love to others. To be in the image of God is to be the embodiment of God's gift of love to others. As God is giver, so am I. Downey's theology is thoroughly relational, which I like, but the movement is all in one direction: from God to us and through us to others.

This works well in giving care to others, but not well in receiving care. I am like God when I give care to others but not when I receive it. Though Downey speaks of giving and receiving within trinitarian relationships, his understanding of divine-human relationships still reflects the medieval view of God as one who gives but does not receive. Thus even in a contemporary relational theology grounded in the Trinity and centered in the gift of love, there is no hint of God receiving what we have to give to God.

Practicing Theology

A whole series of books has been written in recent years on faith practices. Rather than the traditional method of practical theology, which begins with theological formulations and applies the doctrine or teaching to practical situations, this approach begins with faith practices and then explores the scriptural roots of the practice and how it is expressed in congregational and community ministry. This approach was first set forth in a volume edited by Dorothy Bass on *Practicing Our Faith,* which contains essays on faith practices like hospitality, keeping Sabbath, and honoring the body and then examines the theological grounding for each of them.

Traditional theology, following the lead of Aristotle, made a distinction between theology as a theoretical science with the goal of truth and a practical science with the goal of action. Traditionally theology has been understood primarily as a theoretical science and only secondarily as a practical one. The method of doing theology was to begin with Scripture, from which is derived a set of doctrines (teachings). The systematic way those doctrines are organized is determined by tradition (Orthodox, Catholic, Lutheran), historical context (Reformation, Vatican II), and philosophical frame of reference. Practical theology, the last step in the process, is the application of doctrine to everyday life.

Bass and her colleagues move instead from practice to theory, beginning with activities that compose a Christian way of life, and then providing a theological framework for them. Based on the assumption that you can learn about what people believe through their practices as well as through the doctrines they profess, Bass examines practices of faith that have always been part of the Christian life.

The strength of this approach is that it links theology to practice and gives richer meaning to the abstractions that are often the bane of theological formulations. It's not that theology is ignored. We cannot discern the meaning of faith practices apart from the theology that informs them, nor can we judge the faithfulness of these practices apart from a theology grounded in Scripture. By examining how our daily lives are all tangled up with the things God is doing in the world, a theology that begins from the bottom up rather than the top down complements rather than negates traditional methods of doing theology. That's messy at times, but also rich in fresh understanding.

The practices examined in recent books that take this approach are "the human activities in and through which people cooperate with God in addressing the needs of one another and creation" (from *Practicing Theology: Beliefs and Practices in Christian Life*, edited by Dorothy Bass and Miroslav Volf). The implication is that the Christian way of life is defined by what we do in addressing the needs of others. But what do we do in addressing our own needs? We receive care from others and ask for help when we are in need, which is as much a practice of faith as what we do to meet the needs of others. Though God is in the receiving as much as the giving, books and essays in the fields of pastoral care and practical theology have given scant attention to the faith practice of receiving and asking for help.

Dorothy Bass recently wrote me: "I thought you might be interested in the fact that one of the features of CHRISTIAN practice, as I understand it, is the quality of RECEPTIVITY. Thus, we don't try to MASTER the stranger; rather, in Christian hospitality we RECEIVE her. We don't fool ourselves that we can MASTER time with our Palm Pilots; rather, we grow into the acknowledgment that we RECEIVE time as a gift from day to day. It sounds to me as if your work may have a kindred orientation."

Throughout my professional career, my teaching, research, and writing has been in the area of practical theology. I have focused on the church's ministry of health and healing as well as on faith development as it shapes the faith practices of Christians at different stages of life. It was in the latter years of my tenure at Valparaiso University, when Dorothy Bass was just beginning what is now known as The Valparaiso Project, that I was introduced to this new approach to doing practical theology. This shaped the way I thought about receiving care from the beginning of writing this book.

My contribution to the innovative way of doing practical theology that Bass pioneered is the emphasis in this book on receiving as a faith practice. I emphasize receptivity as a quality of being not only in relation to God, but to others as well. This fits with Bass's approach, as she indicates, but I think that in future volumes of the Practices of Faith Series, more attention needs to be given to receiving as a primary feature of Christian practice.

Receiving God's grace is clearly an act of faith. Receiving from others is also a practice of faith, as truly as keeping Sabbath or honoring the body. It is an activity that "Christian people do together over time in response to and in the light of God's active presence for the life of the world," which is the definition of Christian practice that Bass and Craig Dykstra offer in their description of this way of doing theology from the bottom up.

The activity of care-receiving is the Christian practice that forms the basis for the theological reflections in this chapter. Beginning with a sermon based on the theological premise that God gives and never receives, we will take a fresh look at care-receiving as a practice of faith grounded in the God of our receiving.

A Sermon on Giving and Receiving

To illustrate a theology of God as giver but not receiver, I turn to a carefully crafted baccalaureate sermon given by President Mark Hopkins of Williams College in August of 1852. I do so because my focus in this study is on practical rather than academic theology, with preaching and pastoral care rather than scholarly research.

The text of Hopkins's sermon is from Acts 20:35: "It is more blessed to give than to receive." The words are those of Jesus, according to St. Paul, though they are found nowhere in the Gospels. It is a favorite text of preachers who use it regularly to motivate congregations toward greater stewardship and service. It is a text that is invariably referred to in discussions I've had with Christians about receiving care.

Far from denigrating the act of receiving, Hopkins notes that "as a dependent being, man is, and must be, a receiver." Given that fact, "we should anticipate, from the goodness of God, that it would be blessed for him to receive.... It is blessed for the child to receive from the parent, for the friend to receive from his friend. It is always blessed to receive when the gift is born of affection."

Having affirmed the blessedness of receiving, Hopkins moves quickly to the obvious point of every sermon that I've heard or read on this text: that it is more blessed to give. He makes the point by reference to Jesus, who knew the blessings of receiving but "came, not to be ministered unto, but to minister, and to *give* his *life* a ransom for many." As Jesus did, so did the apostles, and so should we, because "to give is more blessed than to receive."

Hopkins grounds this assertion in the theological formulation that "God is a giver only, and not a receiver.... We must conceive of God as self-sufficing in all respects, as having within himself the spring of his own activity...[from which] he manifests himself only as a giver.... Throughout the universe there is nothing that any being is, or that he possesses, that is not the gift of God...The highest conception we can form of any being, that he should not only have the spring of activity within himself and be self-sufficing, but that he should suffice for a universe, and find a conscious blessedness in giving without limit and without exhaustion forevermore."

"And while God thus gives," Hopkins continues, "he does not receive." God may accept our services, but "we can bestow upon him no gift; he can receive nothing from us so as to become the owner of that which was not his before.... If then God finds his own blessedness in giving, and not at all in receiving, we should naturally expect that those who are made in his image would find it more blessed to give than to receive." Hopkins's logic suggests that those who are made *in the image of God* find their blessedness only in giving, and not at all in receiving.

There are many sermons on this text that follow Hopkins's logic and suggest, as does the Lord Bishop of Chester in 1709, that receiving is never more than selfish desire in the service of sin. "Receiving is an argument of emptiness and want; giving, on the contrary, of fulness (sic) and abundance...receiving of a stingy self-love, justly abhorred and despised by everybody, giving of an heroic love of all mankind, as justly esteemed and honored by all." An extreme statement to be sure, but it reflects an attitude that is deeply rooted in Christian self-understanding and practice.

It is difficult for Christians to ask for or receive graciously the care that others offer when the tradition from which they come provides such poor counsel to them. Worse yet is that there is no model for gracious receiving in God's being and doing. How can children receive graciously without a model of such behavior in their parents? How can the children of God receive care graciously without a model of such behavior in their Father/Mother/Creator God?

God as the Ground of Our Receiving

The assertion that God only gives and never receives contradicts scriptural testimony and our experience of being in relation to God. There is close to a consensus among contemporary theologians on this point, few if any of whom would defend the medieval doctrine of God portrayed in Hopkins's sermon. Current scholarship in trinitarian theology on "God as communion" provides not only a critique of Hopkins's understanding of God as only giver but also lays the foundation for speaking of God as the ground of our receiving.

The central biblical affirmation that supports this relational view is that "God is love." All of the initiative in the relationship between God and us comes from God: "In this is love, not that we loved God but that he loved us" (1 John 4:10). Since God loves us, we with grateful hearts are to share that love with others, as Scripture reminds us again and again. But we also love God, because God's love, freely given to us, prompts us to love God in return. Relationships are by definition mutual; so is grace, which moves both ways in any relationship, be that human, divine, or human and divine.

God as Communion

It is the relational component that is missing in the classic doctrine of God. Downey's depiction of love in trinitarian relationships, which is not only interpersonal within the persons of the Trinity but flows from the Trinity to humanity, goes a long way toward correcting a doctrine of God that portrays God as self-sufficient and needing nothing from outside of God's self. Downey's use of relational categories to describe trinitarian relationships and the relationship between God and the world is refreshing, but it falls short of an understanding of God as communion in that it depicts all the movement as one way from God to humanity.

Ted Peters, one among an increasing number of theologians who have recently been using relational categories to rethink the doctrine of the Trinity, states clearly the difference between this approach and the classic Christian doctrine of God:

> The concept of the Trinity has become a weapon in the contemporary war against classical metaphysics - that is, against the classical philosopher's deity that is a se, immutable and unrelated to the world. What characterizes the Christian view, many contemporary theologians seem to agree, is that the God of Jesus Christ is inextricably and passionately involved in the affairs of human history and that this involvement is constitutive of the trinitarian life proper. The current agenda is how to make this comprehensible. (From *God as Trinity: Relationality and Temporality in Divine Life*.)

Karl Barth's seminal insight that God's eternal being must be the same as the God revealed in history was a primary impetus for another look at trinitarian theology. According to Peters and others, God could not be a monad within God's own being and then become relational through interaction with the creation. God must have been relational all along. There must be a correspondence between God's life with the world and the divine life apart from the world. The ancient doctrine of the Trinity, when viewed through the lens of relational categories, provides an avenue for drawing out the implications of Barth's insight.

The eternal nature of God's love is evident within the trinitarian relations of God as Father, Son, and Holy Spirit. As Peters puts it, "The love with which the Father loves the Son and that the Son reciprocates is also the love through which God loves the world and the love that, through the Holy Spirit, is poured into the hearts of those who have faith. This love makes us one with another and with God, just as the Father is one with the Son and the Son with the Father."

Christians have always affirmed that God is most fully revealed to us through the life, death, and resurrection of Christ; yet God remains a mystery beyond the grasp of our most sophisticated theological formulations. Conscious of the limits of our language in speaking of God, medieval theology consistently distinguished between God as Godself (self-sufficient, independent, and ineffable) and God acting in history (involved and interactive). This has meant, as Patricia Fox has noted, "that for a millennium and a half, the doctrine of the Trinity has largely been restricted to consideration of the immanent Trinity (God as Godself). By this century Karl Rahner could make his oft-quoted remark that one could dispense with the doctrine of the Trinity and the major part of religious literature would remain virtually unchanged."

When you think about God from the perspective of Jesus' death and resurrection, the classical attributes for God (independent, immutable, impassable, and apathetic) simply do not ring true. The death and resurrection of Jesus reveal God as unconditional love in solidarity with suffering humanity. But suffering is linked to transiency, contingency, and finitude, conditions of human existence, but terms that are never applied to God. Thus, starting with Aquinas, scholasticism regarded suffering as a state of vulnerability incompatible with divine nature. Jesus could suffer according to his human nature, but not according to his divine nature. The sharp distinction between God as Godself and God acting in history is matched by an equally sharp split between the divine and human nature of Jesus.

This solves a dilemma in how to speak about a God who is fully incarnate and at the same time remote and completely self-sufficient, but it does not do justice to the rich scriptural descriptions of God in Christ, totally immersed in the human condition. Barth said no to the artificial distinction between a distant God and the God whose suffering in Christ is the deepest expression of love that we know. To their credit, contemporary theologians have gone beyond the artificial abstraction between divine and human nature and have chosen instead to re-image God as communion and suffering love.

The key to understanding God as communion and suffering love without diminishing God's power is to combine the two, as Patricia Fox has done with the phrase "relational power":

> The image of an impassible God that enshrines unilateral power as an ultimate goal and derides vulnerability as weakness and imperfection has begun to be replaced by images of a God of relational power that are congruent with scriptural and doctrinal witness. A restored contemporary trinitarian theology holds that the touchstone against which to test every image is the dynamic *koinonia* of love between the divine persons at the heart of the triune symbol. That in turn has led to the need for a resymbolization of divine power as relational power.
>
> Relational power stands in direct contrast to the unilateral power communicated by the omnipotent God of classical theism.... That is the power revealed by a trinitarian God of mutual relations whose very being is communion. It is not a power that has to control; it is a power that emanates from persons who are free to love. It is free to be vulnerable to the limits of the other and to let new life come into being as it will. It is a power that is free enough to enter into suffering. Since love entails suffering, a retrieval of the symbol of the triune God who is love must include images of a God who suffers. (From *God as Communion*.)

Does this mean that God receives as well as gives? I think it does, though it is typical of almost every exposition of God as relational that this is nowhere made explicit. As the importance of receiving is ignored (not denied) in the pastoral care literature, so also in this revised understanding of God as relational. It is yet another example of the scant attention given to receiving gifts, receiving love, receiving care. Relational power is always reciprocal, I would argue, even as grace is always mutual.

The Mutuality of Love and Grace

There are many reasons why grace is consistently defined in Christian theology as unilateral rather than mutual; some of them are noted in this chapter. Those of us reared in the Pauline/Augustinian/Lutheran tradition, with its emphasis on "grace alone," are likely to be particularly sensitive on this issue and quick to object to any suggestion that grace is not unilateral.

For example, Luther insisted that faith is totally the gift of God. He took this position in the Reformation debate over infant baptism to avoid even the slightest suggestion that faith might be considered a "work," something we contribute to a saving relationship with God. Along with his fellow reformers, Luther rejected the Roman Catholic notion of infused grace and affirmed instead that faith is the receiving instrument of God's grace. Those who became known as Baptists followed the logic of this position and postponed baptism until the age of discretion. Not Luther. He argued for infant baptism and infant faith, but he insisted that faith was God's act, grace alone.

Luther's position is the clearest and most extreme illustration I know of unilateral grace that still insists on faith as a human response to the gift of grace. Luther had it right, even though he insisted that faith is completely God's gift and compared the human reception of the gift to a "mathematical point," too minuscule to observe. Very few professional theologians or parish pastors transcend that view. Every sermon I've ever heard on the parable of the prodigal son uses this story of undeserved and unconditional love to convey a message about God's unilateral grace. It seems obvious from a human perspective that the father in this parable received and was blessed by the grateful love of his son, but the implications of that for understanding God as Father are ignored, so deeply ingrained is the view that grace is unilateral.

A relational understanding of God offers welcome support to an image of God as immanent, vulnerable, and suffering in an unwavering and unconditional love for us, but it does not support the affirmation that God is the ground of our receiving. As with so many doctrinal propositions, this view of God is true in what it affirms, but misleading in what it ignores.

In a separate publication I have argued that what Luther lacked in his exposition of infant baptism was a developmental view of faith. If trust is the first developmental stage of faith as it is for human development, then it makes sense to say that in the ritual of initiation God's grace and love literally call the infant into being as a child of God in a way similar to a mother calling an infant into being as her child through the love she showers on her beloved. The focus, as it should be, is on the action of God and mother, but in both cases the response of trust from the infant makes the relationship mutual.

At their best, loving relationships among humans are mutually enlivening. A relationship may be one-sided when one of the parties is extremely vulnerable and needy, as in parent-child relationships and some therapeutic relationships, but even in such extreme situations, relationships are impoverished if the giver receives nothing in return. Surely that is equally true in our relationship to God. What we know about God's relational power in stories about Jesus and God's covenant with Israel reveals relationships that are mutually enlivening, relationships in which God receives as well as gives.

The Relational God of Scriptures

The sermon by Mark Hopkins earlier in this chapter is on solid biblical ground in arguing that God is the gift-giver on whom we are totally dependent for life and salvation. Hopkins is also on solid ground when he preaches, as countless preachers have before and since, that "it is better to give than receive," and that we reflect God's image most clearly when we, too, are gift-givers. However, he lacks biblical support when he argues that God could never be the ground of our receiving because God is only giver and never in need of anything that God might receive from us.

A review of biblical narratives about the action of God in the history of Israel, in the person of Christ, and in the life of the church reveals a deeply relational God who receives as well as gives. This is implicit in the covenants between God and Israel. It is explicit in the story of Jesus who begins life as a dependent child in need of care and who ends life feeling deprived of both God's care and the care of his disciples. In the covenants between God and Israel, and even more so in God's relationship to us in Jesus, we find a pattern of mutual giving and receiving between God and humanity.

Roberta Bondi makes this point convincingly at the conclusion of her account of the mutual giving and receiving of care between herself and her Auntie Ree. After noting how difficult it is for most people to receive care as graciously as her aunt does, Bondi reflects on the theological implications.

> Perhaps this is why certain theological approaches to God want to insist that God needs nothing from us, that God is the only one who can give, while everything we have to give already belongs to God anyway. To think of God as above being able to receive our gifts keeps us aware at all times that our relationship with God isn't really based in the mutuality of love so much as it is based in God's unspeakable power and glory, and in our deplorable weakness and sin.

This is not, however, the baby Jesus, who receives gifts of gold, frankincense, and myrrh; or the adult Jesus, either, who receives the gift of perfume from a woman who pours it over his feet, as well as friendship and consolation from Martha and Mary. In the Old Testament, too, God is offered and gladly receives sacrifices, of heifers, wheat, and praise by those who love God, and the hearts of God's lovers are strengthened and gladdened in return.

Of course, mutuality is not equality in relation to God any more so than in the relationship of parents to children. So dominant is our experience of receiving in relation to God, that it is no wonder that we think of God exclusively as gracious giver of all that is good, and ourselves only as receivers and not mutual givers of that goodness. Rarely do we consider that in Jesus we have a model of receiving as well as giving care.

The Neediness of Jesus

Not all those in need of care receive it graciously, but the evidence we have from the Gospels is that Jesus did. We don't know much about the infancy and early years of Jesus' life, but we know enough about infants to know that Jesus was needy and vulnerable, totally dependent on the protection and care of Mary and Joseph. We have every reason to believe that he not only needed that care and protection, but received it graciously. Artists' portrayals of Jesus in the arms of Mary at the beginning as well as at the ending of his life (Michelangelo's *Pieta*) are realistic portrayals of the care received by Jesus throughout his life.

One could argue that the neediness of Jesus tells us nothing about a God who is transcendent, whose divine nature is sharply differentiated from the human nature of a baby boy. But if God is in the dying, God is also in the birthing. No Christian doubts that God is in the dying; it's the helplessness of the baby that gives us pause. But the baby is God with us as truly as the Christ who died and rose again. We can, with confidence, find the ground of our receiving, as well as our giving, in the God whom we know in Christ as a helpless infant.

It is possible to affirm the baby's divinity while ignoring his neediness. An example is the following portrayal of the infant Jesus in a book of Advent devotions: "It is true that the span of an infant's arms is absurdly short; but if they are the arms of the Divine Child, they are as wide as the reach of the arms on the cross. They embrace and support the whole world; their shadow is the noon-day shade for its suffering people; they are the spread wings under which the whole world shall find shelter and rest."

Besides straining the imagination, this picture of an infant's arms "as wide as the reach of the arms on the cross" distorts a vivid image of Jesus' *receiving* care and converts it to one in which he is *providing* care for the whole world.

Mary Lou Kownacki is more faithful to the image of the infant Jesus and his caring mother in her *Prayer with Mary.* Mary prays, and we with her: "Give me such hospitality of heart that family, foreign seers, poor shepherds, and animals find a home in my presence. Let me protect innocent children from oppressive power. Make me fearless of foreign lands and unknown journeys. When I cannot find you, do not let me rest until I search home, highway, and temple. Let me always insist on miracles to celebrate love. And when all I love on earth lies lifeless in my arms, let me offer it to you with such freedom of heart that I am swept up into the heavens." In this beautiful prayer Mary is the caring one, and Jesus the one receiving care from the beginning to the end of his life.

The dependency of Jesus on his parents' care is not the point of any of the infancy narratives, and quite the opposite of the point in the boy-in-the-temple story, but it hardly needs to be argued that Jesus needed as much care as any other child. Nor did his need for care end with childhood. Jesus calls his disciples friends rather than servants; friends receive as well as give while servants only do as they are told. Jesus' agony is evident when Peter denies him and the rest of the disciples desert him in the hour of his greatest need. Among his closest relationships were those with Mary, Martha ,and Lazarus. The message he receives from the sisters—"Lord, he whom you love is ill" (John 11:5)—draws him to their side to restore a relationship treasured by all four. Several references in the Gospels tell us of women who accompanied Jesus and the disciples, women "who provided for them out of their resources" (Luke 8:3).

The neediness of Jesus tells us nothing is most obvious in the last week of his life. The story of the woman who anoints Jesus with costly ointment (Mark 14:3-9) pictures a Jesus who is grateful for a human act of kindness that strengthened his spirit just days before the end of his life. Mark and Matthew depict Jesus in Gethsemane as greatly distressed and troubled (Mark 14:33). He needs his disciples to stay awake and support him as he grieves his impending death. His disappointment in finding them asleep not once but three times is evidence of an unmet need. This pales, however, in comparison to the anguish Jesus feels in being forsaken by God on the cross. Was Jesus needy? Of course he was. Was God needy? Dietrich Bonhoeffer suggests as much in these moving words from *Letters from Prison:* "Men go to God when he is sore bestead, Find him poor and scorned, without shelter or bread, whelmed under weight of the wicked, the weak, the dead: Christians stand by God in his hour of grieving."

Jesus receives as well as gives. He welcomes children and says that we are to receive God's gifts as children receive them. He is depicted in the Gospels as vulnerable and in need of care. He prays in time of need. He asks support from his disciples. His neediness is deepened by bearing the burden of those who are needy. "In all their affliction he was afflicted" (Isaiah 63:9). He will say one day to those who provided care for the needy, "As you did it to one of the least of these who are members of my family, you did it to me" (Matthew 25:40).

We hear little about this side of Jesus in the liturgy, in sermons, and in prayers. The one exception is during Lent, when the vulnerability and neediness of Jesus cannot be ignored in stories leading to his suffering and death. In churches using the liturgy of the Mass, the triumphant hymn of praise is omitted, and the glorious proclamation of Christ's victory over sin and death awaits Easter. The drama of Lent evokes empathy with the suffering of Jesus and enables those who immerse themselves thoroughly in the Lenten journey to see the image of a vulnerable Jesus in people who need their help, and to know that in caring for them they care for Jesus.

A young man shared with me an intense longing to care for Jesus. He was visiting a Roman Catholic Church in Ireland. There was a large crucifix in the church that was graphic in its depiction of the suffering of Jesus—blood oozing from nails and spear thrust, a crown of thorns, a pained and anguished face, and a body contorted by suffering. As a Protestant, his preference was for a plain cross rather than a crucifix, which he thought could easily become an object of veneration and thus an idol. But he was transfixed by the image on the cross and drawn into the experience to such a degree that he felt as if he were part of the scene. He imagined giving Jesus something to drink, cooling his forehead with a wet cloth, and offering him comfort. He had a strange and powerful feeling that Jesus was comforted by what he was doing, that he was giving his love to Jesus even as he was receiving the benefits of Jesus' sacrificial love.

This young man's active imagination evoked a genuine personal experience of Jesus' both giving and receiving care. It's sad that there are so few stories like his, at least ones that people are willing to share. It goes without saying that images of Jesus caring for others should be much more plentiful in our worship and daily life than images of Jesus receiving care. It is the almost complete absence of the latter that is problematic, especially for those of us (all of us) who need to be assured of the goodness of our receiving, the godliness of it.

Images of Jesus receiving care make sense only within what Luther called a theology of the cross as distinguished from a theology of glory. The latter is centered in a revelation of God's power and majesty, as for example in the giving of the law to Moses on Mt. Sinai. The view of God on the mount of Sinai is strikingly different from the view of God on the mount of Calvary, where we can see only a "hidden God" revealed in a helpless and forsaken figure on the cross. Jesus dreaded this awful death and prayed in Gethsemane that he would be spared from the burden of suffering. Jesus did not receive what he asked for, but he did ask for what he needed, and he did receive an answer to his prayer: care from an angel sent by God to strengthen him for what lay ahead. His agonized cry of desolation from the cross was hardly a demonstration of God's power and glory to those who witnessed it. With Easter vision, however, we can see the "hidden God" in the forsakenness of Jesus acting with power to save all of humanity. This is a God whose receiving did not need to be hidden in this most powerful expression of love and caring that the world has ever witnessed.

A theology of the cross declares that the God who saves is the God who suffers. The clearest image we have of God in all of Scripture is the image of Christ when he was most vulnerable and needed care. The shadow of the cross is cast all the way back to the infant lying in a manger. Nothing could be further from the God that Hopkins depicts as totally transcendent and self-sufficient.

Conclusion

During all the stages of my adult life I managed quite well with a theology of grace that taught me to see myself as receiver in my relation to God and giver in relation to others. It made perfect sense. God freely loves and forgives me, enabling me to love and forgive others freely. I had a clear sense of self in both relationships. In time of need I could cast all my care on God who cares for me. As a husband, a father, a pastor, a counselor, and a professor, I mediated the care of God to others.

Though I experienced my share of struggles and disappointments through the years, I could, for the most part, hide my vulnerability from others, even from myself. I learned what every child learns through the process of socialization: that to be an adult is to become independent and to provide for others. As a male child, I learned to do so with little, if any, admission of neediness on my part. I learned the lesson well—too well. And I had a theology that supported it, including the image of a Father God who is self-sufficient. The more caring I was and the more self-sufficient, the closer I was to an image of God who is all-caring and completely self-sufficient.

Awareness of my vulnerability deepened after the diagnosis of cancer. I could go to God with my neediness, but I found it agonizingly difficult to acknowledge this need to others. It was not that God's unconditional love and forgiveness was overemphasized; I rely on God more than ever. But my theology had not taught me that God is in the receiving, as well as the giving, of care; it had not given me Jesus as a model for gracious care-receiving. I had not learned that I reflect the image of God when I'm vulnerable as well as when I'm strong.

We need a theology that supports the practice of receiving care as well as giving it. I know through many conversations that this need is shared by others. We need to affirm the goodness of needing care, to affirm our vulnerability as a core element in the human condition, to confess that God so created us, and to recognize our strength in acknowledging dependency.

We are created in the image of a loving God who became totally vulnerable so that the world could be redeemed. This God, whom we know in Christ, understands our vulnerability and neediness. This God is at one with us in receiving care from our sisters and brothers, as well as in providing them with care.

chapter three

STORIES OF RESISTANCE AND GRACE IN RECEIVING CARE

Abba James said, "It is better to receive hospitality than to offer it." —The Sayings of the Desert Fathers

Social science research (Chapter 4) and theological reflection about receiving care (Chapter 2) offer helpful insights for both providers and recipients of care, but nothing stimulates the imagination more than stories about the experience of receiving care. Good preaching is peppered with good stories. The parables of Jesus, such as the story of the good Samaritan, give more insight into caregiving than the heady theological formulations of St. Paul. The stories in this chapter are modern parables about the experience of receiving care.

We do not lack for stories about people who provide care. The care providers are the heroes, highly regarded for their selfless devotion. Stories of Mother Teresa caring for the dying poor in

India are an inspiration to all who hear them. So are stories about Albert Schweitzer, the fabled physician, who was well known for his genius in music and theology, yet devoted his life to the care of impoverished peasants in an obscure mission station. These are the saints whom parents admire and hope their children might one day emulate in lives of service and care for those in need.

Receivers of care, on the other hand, are more likely to be regarded with pity. Their stories rarely get told unless their need to be heard prompts them to publish an account of their experience. The best stories I could find on the experience of receiving care came from autobiographies of the handicapped, the chronically ill, and the frail elderly, a select population of people who have experienced extended periods of vulnerability and extreme dependence. I will rely heavily on quotations from these autobiographies. In addition, I've relied heavily on personal experience and workshop accounts.

We need to hear these stories of the vulnerable and dependent among us. They know what it's like to receive care, both good and bad. The stories you'll read in this chapter are mostly from severely dependent adults in need of more care and for longer periods than any of us are ever likely to experience. Most of us would not hesitate to tell stories of receiving care in good times, times when we are able to reciprocate, but not many of us are willing to share stories of receiving care when we are vulnerable, dependent, and unable to reciprocate.

Most of the stories in this chapter are about the difficulty of receiving care and asking for help. It's not that people aren't grateful for the care they receive, but their experience is generally more negative than positive. Why not more stories about receiving care graciously? I've looked for them in autobiographies and asked for such stories in workshops and personal conversations, but there aren't many, and a surprising number of them are about someone other than the narrator.

We are barely conscious of the social rules we follow in giving and receiving care until we encounter a situation where the rules don't work or aren't clear. Those who have long experience with receiving care in time of need can show us the limits of these rules and teach us to become better care receivers in our own time of need and better caregivers as well. Pay close attention to your emotional response to these stories as a gauge of your receptivity to receiving care.

The goal of listening carefully to these stories is not only to overcome the innate resistance to receiving care but also to find satisfaction in a growing capacity to receive care graciously.

Resistance to Receiving Care

My brother discussed the topic of receiving care with a group of Stephen Ministers who provide care to members of their congregation. He reports: "If there was some consensus at the end of the discussion, it was that people tend to keep problems to themselves, and when their problems are known, they tend to resist care offered by others, thinking they should be able to handle them on their own."

This observation was confirmed again and again in stories I've elicited and read in autobiographies. Most people admit to an intuitive, almost automatic resistance to receiving care. I asked a group of workshop participants about this, and the response of one of them was typical of many others: "I hated being sick and needing care. I was very anxious to get well enough to take over. I took over before the doctor said I could. I didn't like receiving care—it embarrassed me. I asked for the minimum needs. I felt the person caring for me must get tired and frustrated and wish to go home. I thought she didn't believe I really needed help—that I was malingering."

What makes it so hard to receive care?

I asked groups of about 40 participants in a number of workshops to list the things that made it difficult for them to receive care. The most frequently repeated reasons were:

1. Turning over control of one's care to another (17)
2. Fear of dependency (14)
3. Pride (12)
4. Not wanting to impose on others (11)
5. Role reversal from caregiver to care receiver (8)

Other reasons cited more than once were: embarrassment; lack of self-worth; fear of giving up; lack of trust; no opportunity to return the favor; risk of exposure; prior experience with incompetent and insensitive caregivers; lack of practice; loss of privacy; and discomfort with so much attention.

A common thread among all these responses is a loss of self-sufficiency and self-worth. Receiving care means you are not worth much to yourself or anybody else beyond a small circle of family and friends, and it's not always obvious (at least to you) that you're worth much to them either.

One of the reasons cited above—not wanting to impose on others—might be interpreted as further evidence of low self-worth. A more likely explanation is that resistance to having a loved one sacrifice so much time, effort, and money is an expression of love. Concern for those who provide one's care is evidence of mutuality in caring and receiving, and thus a strength to be encouraged rather than a weakness that needs to be overcome.

How strange that the care which is absolutely essential for survival in childhood and deeply cherished in healthy relationships is perceived by many adults, especially older adults, almost as a curse when the need for it is greatest. I've explored this topic with many individuals and groups over the past few years, and there is little variation in a common lament about the difficulties in receiving care. Unless we understand the depth of that feeling and some of the reasons for it, little can be done to shape a more positive attitude about receiving care graciously.

Some of the factors contributing to resistance
to receiving care

Denial is a common defense against negative feelings about receiving care. A striking example is the consistent use of denial by Robert Murphy in *The Body Silent*. Murphy, a prominent anthropologist, is a quadriplegic as a result of progressive paralysis. He uses his skills as a cultural anthropologist to describe his gradual decline in physical mobility and what that has taught him about the social relations of persons who are disabled.

A glaring absence in his otherwise insightful narrative is any reference to the experience of receiving care. There are detailed descriptions of his increasing need for help, particularly from his wife, when he had reached the point of almost complete disability. Yet he says nothing about the experience, how hard or easy it was for him to ask for help, or what he perceived to be the effect on his wife. This is from a learned anthropologist who is trained in observation and likely aware of the research literature in the social sciences on receiving care.

Murphy sees himself as a lone hero who fights valiantly for maintenance of self-worth and productivity, a hero with a "can do" attitude that most Americans would applaud. Yet he is a *lone* hero, and that's the shadow side of this powerful drama of a strong and self-sufficient man piloting his ship through a withering storm of adversity.

To cite but one of many examples, he describes his experience of a heart attack, a time when he was in desperate need of help. He gives a bare-bones account of this situation in a single sentence: "Since most of my family live near by, they took care, not only of me but paying my bills, getting any medicine, etc. that I needed and taking me to the doctor for check-ups." Nothing about the experience of receiving care, nothing about how it felt to be so completely dependent on family members for the help he needed, nothing about what they received from him in the extended period of rehabilitation from a life-threatening crisis.

Incompetent and insensitive caregivers heighten resistance to receiving care. A patient recovering from hip surgery was assigned a home-care worker to provide 20 hours of assistance with bathing, shopping, laundry, cleaning, and meal preparation each week. The first time the assigned worker visited, she told him that because she lived an hour away and received no mileage reimbursement, she expected him to sign a dishonest time sheet: 20 hours pay for nine hours of work! Desperate for help, he reluctantly agreed. Angry at being blackmailed, he became testy and irritable, especially when she bathed him. "I felt humiliated by having someone else perform this intimate act, and hated feeling helpless and vulnerable, emotions that were exacerbated when Miriam made remarks about my scars or appearance."

Excessive solicitude can be as insensitive as caring too little. Hector Chevigny describes the first time he left the hospital on his own after a traumatic loss of his sight. Badly in need of a haircut and shave, he called a hotel barbershop, explained that he was blind and that he would be arriving by taxi. He thought the rest would be simple. When he arrived, the manager and two bellboys ushered him up the back way. The barbershop grew hushed as he entered. He made a joke about having a haircut every three months whether he needed it or not. Nobody laughed. The bellboys literally lifted him into the barber's chair.

Jacob Neusner, a distinguished scholar of Jewish studies, argues that *how* one gives matters at least as much as *what* one gives: "What is required is consideration for the humanity of the recipient who remains no different from the donor. Those who receive are not less than or different from those who give. They have not only needs but also feelings. They welcome not only the beneficence of the wealthy but also their respect. So the act of giving should be done in such a way that acknowledges the equality of the giver and the receiver. The religious imperative is not just an act of grace or even an expression of caring. It is for the faithful both an expression of duty and an act of respect."

Loss of independence is a loss of freedom and self-sufficiency, and at least to some degree a loss of control over events in our lives. We are never fully independent, of course, nor would we wish to be, but we do hope for an appropriate balance between dependence and independence, giving and receiving.

It's when the balance is lost because of excessive dependence that receiving care becomes especially hard. Hector Chevigny describes his initial experience at the sudden onset of adult blindness:

> The full realization of my future dependence on people now descended on me. ... It was a surprise to discover that I so valued my independence; its loss now seemed all but impossible of acceptance. The thought of being forever under the necessity of asking someone, even someone close and dear to me, for the privilege of movement was a pill almost too bitter to swallow. And what right did I have to impose this burden on the world? By what arrogant standard was my life so precious that I could demand the price of its existence from others?

In even stronger language, a man whose lung condition made him breathless after just a few steps says: "I can't drive anymore and I can't get on the damn bus, but you're crazy if you think I'm gonna bug my daughter each time I need a quart of milk. That's all there is to it. You go because you have to, because you want to be in charge of your life."

Some people will go to great lengths to regain loss of control that comes with dependence. A young woman describes her recovery from illness as a struggle to regain control: "When I went home after 15 days in the hospital, the first thing I needed to accomplish was getting my kitchen in order. I sat in a chair in the middle of the kitchen and directed my mom and a friend of mine in putting things back in 'proper order.' I had felt so out of control."

One of the most traumatic events in the lives of older adults is no longer being able to drive. Even when someone is available and willing to provide transportation, the transition to a time of increasing dependence is excruciating for people who have, throughout their adult lives, been active and productive. I heard and read many stories of people who chose to stay home rather than being dependent on others.

The tension between dependence and autonomy is a lifelong issue. We begin life in the womb, and in early childhood are totally dependent on those who care for us. We struggle for independence in adolescence. We fight its loss in our declining years. A poem by Claire Bateman, *Childhood of a Stranger,* captures this movement better than prose or any single story:

> You too once were carried in your sleep—
> You to someone a warm weight of breath and cloth,
> Wisps of sleep like slow steam off your seamless face,
> Day distilling into dreams in a skull yet soft.
> Now we are encrusted with barbed years,
> Flinty, adamantine, ready to repel
> All assaults against our independence.
> But for that hint of honey, trace of down,
> That secret nerve that never has grown numb,
> There is a debt between us even now
> That our autonomy cannot remove:
> A bent toward something more than tolerance,
> Older than kindness, oddly akin to love.

Resisting care from one's children is common when the children become the caregivers and parents the recipients of care, a reversal of roles that is fraught with tension and potential conflict. In such cases, parental pride can be a major obstacle to receiving care. Children who are frustrated by their parents' resistance to receiving care may in time come to identify with those feelings. So it was with this elderly woman:

> My mother had nine children, but she refused to live with any of us. We did some of her errands, but she hardly let us help her at all. I was mad at her, because I thought it was foolish pride. Now I know what she was doing. It's hard to depend on your children, and it's hard not to. You have your pride, but you need the help. It's a fine line. When I hear myself saying "no, thanks" to my daughter, I know what was going through my mother's mind back then.

In a parent-child relationship marked by the absence of expressions of appreciation for care-receiving, it may be difficult to recognize care when it is offered. Robert Bly tells the story of a young man, the son of a mechanic, who with the family's help became a college professor. When his father fell gravely ill, the son called to offer his support and sympathy. "Hi, Dad, it's John." The father replies, "Wait, I'll call your mother." "No, Dad, I want to talk to you." Puzzled, the father says, "Do you want something?" "No," the son replies, "but I have been thinking how hard you worked so that I could get an education, and how grateful I am to you. I wanted to say that I love you." After a pause, the father responds, "Have you been drinking?" A funny yet sad story about a father who could not recognize, much less receive, the care of his son, because it was so unexpected and out of character for both the son and his father.

It is also difficult for a child to receive care from a parent when the offer is unexpected and out of character. My father was a fun-loving person, always kidding around, almost never serious. One of the rare exceptions to this came early in my adolescence when he took me aside, spoke of the dangers of smoking, and urged me never to start. I was literally struck dumb by the gravity of his voice and this rare moment of reaching out to me.

I listened, but said nothing in return. The response he was hoping for did come because of the deep and lasting impression of his concern for me, and I was spared this unhealthy addiction.

The outcome was not so fortunate when the roles were reversed and my father asked me for pastoral care on my last visit before he died. Though in obvious pain, he was able to carry on with his usual banter. He walked with me to the hospital exit, and as we approached the door he turned to me and out of the blue asked for spiritual support, for pastoral care. Though as a pastor I regularly dealt with such situations, this was so completely outside the frame of my relationship to him that I was literally speechless. I stumbled around, embarrassed, and this extraordinary request for care was lost. I can only imagine how difficult it was for him to ask for my help at the very end of our visit and our lifelong relationship. I deeply regret the missed opportunity and often revisit it in my mind, and to this day I pray that he understood how unprepared I was to respond.

The need to repay those who provide care is another source of resistance to receiving care when there is no opportunity to reciprocate. One of the clearest findings in the social science research on care-receiving is a strong need to reciprocate acts of kindness. Anthropological studies indicate that it is a universal human need. In most social transactions, the balance between giving and receiving is maintained with relative ease. Goods are exchanged by means of barter or sale.

Relationships among friends and adult family members are, for the most part, interdependent, each person receiving as well as giving. There are times when the balance can no longer be maintained because one of the parties in the relationship is in need of care that cannot be reciprocated. A temporary imbalance, as in the case of a short-term illness, rarely creates problems because there will be occasions to reverse roles. A permanent imbalance is another matter, and it's one of the most frequently cited reasons why receiving care is so difficult.

The reasoning makes perfect sense. If I can't reciprocate by caring for the person who is caring for me, then I'm a burden with no right to ask for the help I do need. A rural elder interviewed by Eva Salber speaks for many older adults: "The worst thing now is that I can't get to go nowhere, only when somebody come around and take me. I hate to bother children all the time and I hate to bother my friends ... I just hope and pray when I gets sick to die, I hope I'll just die. I don't want to be no trouble to nobody. They have children and a family of their own and they has to work. I don't want to bother them from working."

Most volunteer caregivers would regard payment for their services as inappropriate, but often fail to appreciate that it's not at all inappropriate for the person receiving care. My brother drives people to appointments now and then for an area agency on aging. On one occasion he drove a woman to her doctor's appointment. She wanted to pay him. He said no, this was a service the agency provided. The following week he got money from her in the mail. He sent it back with a note suggesting that she donate it to the charity of her choice. This woman simply couldn't handle *not* reciprocating for a much-needed service. She didn't want to be beholden.

The need to repay can easily become an obligation to be pleasant if there is no other way to reciprocate. Zola states: "After several months of hospitalization, it became clear that there were many ways I was going to be dependent on others. Somehow I had to adapt if I wanted to deserve their help or at least make it easy for them to give it. ... Nice as I was, I would just have to be nicer. A friend recently put this decision into clearer terms. Now that I've got this problem [a degenerative disease], I just can't afford to be angry with anyone. I need them too much."

Overcoming Resistance to Receiving Care

Resistance to receiving care is deep seated, as we all know from personal experience. Relatively rare are stories of people who have overcome that resistance. From them we can glean some of the factors that enable care receivers to overcome their resistance. Becoming aware of the barriers to receiving care is certainly an important first step. Beyond such awareness, there are two closely related challenges that one must meet to be fully ready to receive care. First, we need to be able to ask for the help we need, not just wait until someone provides it. Second, we must be able to accept the inevitable ambivalence that any adult has in receiving care over the long haul.

Learning to ask for help

Small children not only ask for, but demand, what they need, as when infants scream until they are fed. They temper their demands by saying "please" as they grow older, but the asking comes easily and naturally. An adolescent will still ask freely, especially of parents, but not a young adult who has left home and takes pride in his or her self-sufficiency. By middle age we are regarded by others and ourselves as providers, not receivers, and we are likely to feel personally diminished if we have to ask for help. One might think this would change for older adults, who are sometimes as dependent for help as small children, but we do not easily divest ourselves of the myth of self-sufficiency.

I mentioned earlier that I made a fortuitous decision at the time of my cancer diagnosis to share information with family and friends about the disease and how I was coping with it. However, even though it has brought me a ton of support, that's not asking for help. The difference between sharing information and asking for help became a gut-wrenching reality to me after I had lived for four years with bone marrow cancer.

In 2002, lab reports for the first time indicated some disease progression. As usual, I shared this quarterly report with those on my e-mail list and received, as I always did, many spontaneous, heartening messages of support. There was a notable exception, however. For three weeks I heard nothing from two of my three daughters. For the first time, the pattern of report and spontaneous response did not hold. Why had I heard nothing? I received two responses from my son-in-law, but nothing from my daughter. What to do? I needed some indication of their support—not much, just some expression of concern. The solution was obvious: Just call them, tell them how much I love them, and ask for their support. But I couldn't do it. I couldn't bring myself to ask for support from daughters who had just spent a week with me at a lovely resort as a gift for my 70th birthday. It took a week of anguished soul-searching and a talk with a good friend before I could, with great resistance, pick up the phone. So simple to call, so hard to ask for what I needed.

In a recent conversation with a friend about my difficulty in asking for help, I came to see some of the dynamics behind this resistance. As a counselor, I had for years cautioned clients against making decisions for others, that people should be given the respect and trust to respond appropriately to requests for help, but I could never follow the advice myself. Why did it seem so obvious to me in counseling others but not at all obvious in my relationship to others?

I came to see why in reflecting on my past behavior. I've always had trouble in saying no to others, even when it would have been wise and appropriate to say no. I have a desire to please others, to affirm their virtues and ignore their faults. Confrontation makes me uncomfortable, and I rarely do it. I project that onto others and do them the dishonor of assuming that they will act as I would in saying yes when they really meant no.

The insight is accurate, I think, but insight rarely changes behavior. So my daughter, who lives with us, proposed a plan to practice a different response. Once a week I ask her for something that I wouldn't normally request. It can be something as simple as asking her to go into another room to get something for me or asking her to go to a movie with me or read to me. Her response is to be completely honest with me, which comes naturally to her. A typical response to a request for help might be: "No, I can't right now." Or she might respond, "I'd like that, but I need to pick the time because of my shifting schedule." There are many possible responses to a request for help, but I trust her to be fully honest in her responses. That has worked well, but there has been little change in my behavior in asking for what I need from others. There will be more on practices to change such behavior in Chapter 6.

We are so conscious of not wanting to be a burden to others, of wanting to maintain our independence and stay in control, that we fail to be attentive to how honored loved ones can feel when we do ask for help. I once shared with a good friend how difficult it was for me to ask for support when I was feeling down because of my illness. She suggested calling a few people I trusted and asking permission to call them when I felt the need to talk. I did this, and all of them thanked me for making the request, saying how honored they felt that I had asked. I expected them to say yes to my request, but I was more than a little surprised that each expressed so strongly the honor they felt at being asked.

An elderly woman in the myeloma support group I attend shared with us what her pastor said when she refused to ask for help: "Sister, you need to grant us the blessing to grant you care, to be the abiding and healing presence of Jesus for you. It's selfish of you not to grant us that blessing." People easily go to God in time of need, but rarely do they consider that asking for help within the community of faith is a form of praying to God.

Our preoccupation with the difficulty of asking for help blinds us to the honor that is ours to bestow on those who are eager to care for us. A middle-aged son describes his reaction to a request for help from his father:

My father was always the biggest stickler on earth when it came to his checkbook. He never let anyone near it, not even my mother. In his eighties, his hand tremor got really bad, but he still insisted on paying all his bills himself. One day, out of the blue, he called me up and asked me to come over to help him write out checks. I couldn't believe it. I was incredibly nervous when I sat down next to him to do it. I handle million-dollar budgets for my company, and yet my hand started to shake for a lousy checkbook. I guess I wanted to please him, or maybe it was that I felt so honored that he was finally trusting me.

Accepting Ambivalence about Receiving Care

Because the recipient of a gift feels a need to reciprocate, ambivalence about receiving care is inevitable in a long-term relationship of dependency. Contrary feelings of gratitude and resentment can and do exist side-by-side, sometimes so intensely they threaten the relationship on which the care receiver is most dependent for help: "Getting my shirt on in the morning is a big thing for me. My wife sits there while I fumble. It's hard for me to get the sleeve to line up so my arm gets through the hole. It takes her just a second to help me, but if she does I yell at her. And when she doesn't, I resent the hell out of her. How's that for a setup? There's no way for either of us to win."

Even asking for a small favor becomes a momentous decision when you are completely dependent:

During the course of a day, I usually ask Yolanda for dozens of small services, over and above the main care she gives me. Since I know that she is overburdened, I generally hesitate to ask for things and feel slightly guilty about bothering her. ... As a result, I am especially sensitive to the tone of her response. Do I detect a note of impatience? Is she annoyed? Is she overtired?

Should I have asked her? Does that slight inflection say, "What in hell does he want from me now?"

A cancer patient isolated by his illness is torn between a desire to be left alone and a yearning for care: "There I was home in bed, just a terrible burden to everyone. But at the same time I resented them for going on with their lives. I didn't want them to bother, I really wanted to be alone most of the time anyway, but I still wanted them to take care of me. Isn't that crazy?"

Ambivalence in the care receiver evokes feelings of ambivalence in the person providing care. So it was for a woman providing care for an older man: "He acted as though he'd rather that I do not give assistance or talk about his recovery plans. He accepted my efforts with apparent appreciation, but also gave me the impression through word and deed that he 'could have done it himself' when I offered assistance. I felt ambivalent about giving care. I didn't want him to feel dependent or that I was helping 'the sick, old man.' But I still love him and want to make it easier for him."

Ambivalence is a given in a long-term relationship of care giving and receiving, but strong bonds of love can keep it from undermining the relationship. A daughter describes the care she gave her mother in the last years of her life: "Sometimes she resented needing help, but then said that this was now our [her children's] duty to care for her. She did not want to give up control at all, so she continued to give instructions as to what needed to be done and when! Sometimes I resented being told when and how, but I never resented doing for her as much as I could to make her comfortable and happy."

The daughter in this example would not have been able to accept either her own or her mother's ambivalence about their relationship without understanding and thoughtful reflection. You can discern the same qualities in Robert Murphy's description of his changing marital relationship:

My dependency weighs upon her heavily, teasing out all the negative side of connubial ambivalence. ... My reliance on her goes far beyond the norm in marriage, and the care she gives me is less wifely than maternal. She does all the things that a mother does for her child, and we both have reacted against this mutation in our relationship by a measure of repressed antagonism toward each other. I want a wife, not a mother, I say— but she has also remained very much my wife. I really have a wife-mother now.

Murphy was able to accept his ambivalence by reframing his care-receiving experience. A caregiver can do the same, as in this relationship:

She accepted almost every offer of care—only turning it down when she felt she could do it herself. There were times when she said what a burden she was, but seemed to accept it when I assured her that it was my pleasure to be able to be there and be of help and also that some day it would be my turn to be the receiver and that I was sure God would provide for me, too. One time she said she wished she would still be around to be that caregiver. I truly loved being one of the givers, though it was exhausting at times.

The Faith Factor in Embracing the Role of Care Receiver

When I reread this manuscript after the revelatory experience described in the addendum of Chapter 1, I was surprised to find there was so little about faith as a factor in receiving care. In much of my teaching and writing, I had focused on faith as an often-forgotten factor in health and healing.

Chapter 2, "A Theology of Receiving Care," focuses on a revised understanding of God as relational, a God capable of receiving as well as giving, but there was almost nothing in the chapter about faith as the human response to the gracious giving of God.

I was surprised by how much the experience of faith described in Chapter 1 enabled me to more fully embrace my role as care receiver. This includes the changing patterns of the experience of faith. In this particular case, it was the revelatory experience described in Chapter 1 that enabled a reversal of roles from giver of care to receiver of care.

Generally, receiving and asking for help are to dependence what the exercise of power and control is to independence. The tension is between receiving/asking for help and being in control and managing one's life. The stronger the need to be in control, the less can one receive and ask. The opposite is not true.

Dependence is not likely to make it easier to receive if a person has a long-term aversion to receive and ask, as most of us do. The need to be independent, in control, and with sufficient power to achieve what is needed for a full and secure life is the primary mechanism behind the aversion to receiving and asking. If one has sufficient independence and control, as most people do during their adult life, there is little to fear.

The problem comes when independence and control are at risk. If the dependence is short-term, most of us are willing to receive and ask for help in interdependent relationships, knowing that we are likely to be in a position of reciprocating. Receiving and asking during prolonged dependence is a challenge difficult to achieve without some help before the onset of the prolonged dependence.

The personal transformation I experienced in the hospital did more to increase my willingness to receive and ask for help than all the thinking I had done about these matters in writing this manuscript. The shift that had taken place in the center of myself without my making it happen was an experience of faith that was pure receiving from God, a gift that made the phrase "practice of faith" a bit jarring because it had too much of myself in it. The experience of "pure receiving" from God is the standard for all receiving, even though "pure receiving" can be experienced only in relation to God.

It is only in the faith experience of "pure receiving" from God that I can fully recognize the receiving itself as a gift— God's doing and not mine. What surprised me after my revelatory experience was that for the first time this same dynamic of faith was present as I received gifts from others. Nothing else made sense out of the transformation I experienced in receiving and asking for help. It was not that receiving was now something I could do with less resistance, but that the resistance was simply no longer there. Is this new experience of receiving a gift from those who offer help and loving support, or is it a gift from God? I cannot tell where one ends and the other begins, or whether it is meaningful to draw a line between them.

How did I get from resistance to receiving care and asking for help to a greatly reduced resistance that sometimes felt like no resistance at all? I have no logical answer to this question. What is clear to me beyond doubt is that my change of behavior can be traced to the revelatory experience described in the addendum to Chapter 1.

There is so much that conditions us against asking for help, so much ambivalence in the tension between our need for care and our resistance to it. Yet there are times when the resistance breaks down, there are caregivers whose loving presence lowers the barriers, and there are revelatory moments when a shift in self-awareness leads to acceptance of the role of care receiver.

Awareness of Vulnerability and Openness to Receiving Care

Robert Murphy describes such a revelatory moment when the awareness of his vulnerability led to a greater openness to receiving care:

The shell of protection that I had built around my emotions melted, and my defenses—a wall built of humor, acerbity, and cynicism—fell before a welling of emotion that was a total departure from my usual state of mind. ... It seemed that the sharp edges of myself had become porous and weak. People could reach into me more easily, and they, in turn, were more vulnerable to me. I did not set hard borders around my identity; I was suffused with a kind of peacefulness, almost a sense of joy. It was all very strange.

A heightened sense of vulnerability brings a need for support and sometimes even the initiative to seek it out. A man in failing health broke his pattern of isolation by forming a support group of male friends in a similar predicament, a group in which he could give as well as receive. With the support of others, this lonely man became capable of an inner awareness that he had not previously experienced: "All my life I had been forced to focus on externals; to focus on anything else was regarded as idle daydreaming. But the externals, when applied to the stretch of life that now lay ahead of me—aging, old age, a probable terminal illness, death, and a possible world beyond—left me absolutely nothing. ... The inner landscape, once it was really discovered and lived in, was aglow."

Terminal illness heightens a sense of vulnerability as well as readiness to live in the present moment. Cicely Saunders, the founder of hospice care, states: "People who are dying often have a tremendous capacity for meeting ... because they have put aside the mask that we tend to wear in everyday life. Now they are ready to meet, just as themselves, and I am sure this is why you can get to know these patients in an extraordinarily short time."

Our capacity and willingness to receive care graciously must be matched, of course, by those who will freely and graciously provide it. Can we count on that? Wendy Lustbader speaks for us all: "The expectation that we will be able to count on kind-ness during our time of need becomes one of life's most sus-taining convictions. We hope that if we become incapacitated, our friends and relatives will stand by us. We hope that their help will arise out of affection rather than out of pity, and that we will bear our difficulties gracefully enough to keep on inspiring their loyalty. We suspect that the measure of a good life is how we are treated at the end."

Receiving Care Graciously

In an essay on "Giving and Receiving," Freya Stak provides a striking description of gracious care receiving by relating it to the giving of care:

> There is generosity in giving, but gentleness in receiv-ing. ... The common emphasis on giving has indeed helped to destroy the receptive attitude in us all. Yet the one is but a personal luxury, a thing to be earned and worked for, an extra, a garland for one's own head at the feast of life: the other is a part of that general thankful-ness which is worked into the very dough of which our bread is kneaded—it comes with every day of sunshine or night of stars: and gratitude is the greatest tribute which one human being can offer to another, since it is the same as must be offered with every breath of our happiness to God. We feel this unconsciously, and love those people who give with humility, or who accept with ease.

Three necessary if not sufficient indicators of readiness for gracious care-receiving were examined in the previous section on "overcoming resistance to receiving care."

- Asking for help
- Accepting ambivalence
- Embracing the role of care receiver

Each is characteristic of people who have moved beyond their resistance and are prepared to receive care. What then are some of the qualities of people who are able to receive care graciously?

Building relationships

Freely giving and receiving care adds strength to relationships, while resisting care does the opposite. Those who are wise and open to receiving care know that it is in their self-interest to build and strengthen the relationships on which they depend.

A close relative told me about her Aunt Gert, who began immediately building relationships when she moved into a nursing home. Knowing that her memory was failing, she jotted down the names of the women who were her caregivers: nurses, aides, cleaning people, everyone. Instead of "Good morning," it would be "Good morning, Karen." She wanted these women to be more than "the one who brings breakfast," and she wanted to be more than "the woman in 313." She knows something about many lives and families now. And the people on the staff love her.

Though building relationships comes more easily for some than others, it takes a conscious effort when you're feeling unsure of yourself. It is natural to hide your vulnerability by withdrawing into a protective shell and emerging only with gentle coaxing from a gracious caregiver. Gracious care receivers are able to transcend their vulnerability and build relationships grounded in love and mutual care.

Sensitivity to the needs of the caregiver

A sure way to build and strengthen relationships is through sensitivity to the needs of others. Sensitivity is heralded as an asset in those who give care; it is no less so in those who receive it. The difference is that it is easier for caregivers than care receivers to be empathic to the needs of the other. Family and friends spontaneously feel empathic toward those whom they love, and those in helping professions learn its value through training and experience. Not so for care receivers, whose experience of pain and suffering can be so overwhelming that it's virtually impossible to be aware of anything else. In addition, resistance to receiving care adds an additional barrier to whatever capacity for empathy a care receiver may have.

The capacity for empathy is greatly diminished when a caregiver has to become a receiver of care; even when pain and suffering is not an issue. I have had many people comment on my capacity for empathy in caring for others. Now I hear comments from people about my *lack* of sensitivity to the needs of those who are eager to provide care for me. I make the kind of prejudgments about their needs that I would never make as a caregiver—that they have more important things to do, that I would just be a burden, that they are responding to my needs because they feel obligated, and so forth.

Sensitivity to the needs of caregivers can improve the prospects for continued care, especially when the needs of the care receiver are overwhelming. Chevigny describes his stay with friends while attending a school for the blind: "I was a guest. I had to behave like one. I couldn't, in all courtesy, permit them to do more than the most necessary waiting on me. ... I didn't want my friends to feel that I had to be in their apartment day in and out. ... I made as many dates as I could to see acquaintances elsewhere, for lunch, dinner, for the evening."

The difference between Chevigny's independence and the fierce independence of those unwilling to accept help is his sensitivity to the needs of his friends and his recognition that he needs to maintain these relationships to find his way into the future.

That's often the case, as it was with a homebound person whose sensitivity to the needs of her caregivers strengthened her relationship to people on whom she was dependent:

One of my neighbors is full of religion and she just wants me to listen to that stuff while she makes up my bed. Another one just wants me to notice the special things she gets for me when she does my shopping. And there's one that can't stand it if I thank her, so I have to act like the treats she brings me are the most natural things in the world. Each one's different. I like to give them what they want, so they'll keep being good to me.

Commenting on this story, Wendy Lustbader notes: "Successfully handling the needs and anxieties of their helpers frequently becomes a source of strength for dependent people. A disabled man notes how his forthright requests for aid tend to relieve those who are not sure how to approach him: 'Innumerable times I have seen the fear and bewilderment in people's eyes vanish as I have stretched out my hand for help, and I have felt life and warmth stream from the helping hands I have taken'" (*Counting on Kindness*).

Gratitude

Gratitude is what most people mention first if asked about their experience of receiving care, no matter what the source— God, family, friends, pastor, or paid professional. Though many cannot express their gratitude with ease, most people are fully aware of how privileged they are to receive care.

Not all gratitude is gracious. It is often nothing more than the perfunctory "thank you" we are taught to say from early childhood. It may be a grudging acknowledgement of a favor from someone who is otherwise quite disagreeable. Gratitude can be offensive when excessive, as when an obsequious person uses it to curry favor from a person in authority.

Gratitude is a complex dynamic in a relationship of prolonged dependence, a complexity derived from an imbalance between giving and receiving. The Roman historian Tacitus speaks for many when he says, "Services are welcome as long as it seems possible to repay them, but when they greatly exceed that point, they produce not gratitude but hatred" (*The Annals of Imperial Rome*).

The imbalance between giving and receiving generates an expectation of gratitude and a feeling of obligation to give it, both of which are likely to be barriers to gracious caregiving and care-receiving. In his detailed chronicle of living with a disability in an institutional setting, Irving Zola notes that the act of being grateful can be both humiliating and invalidating when it feels forced and comes at the expense of expressions of anger that may also be felt.

Genuine gratitude is often possible only when the receiver of care feels free to say exactly how she feels, as is illustrated in the following story by Karl Lutze, who tells about a phone call he made to a woman in her nineties who had just celebrated a birthday:

> She told me about greeting cards and phone calls and people who dropped by to wish her well. And when she completed her report to me, I asked, "And how are you, Helen?" I heard her sigh. For a moment she said nothing. Then she said, "You know, I love all these people. I don't know what I'd do without them or their love. ... They tell me my 'smiling face and cheery disposition' are contagious and always make their spirits bright. And then you come along. And you don't require anything of me. You take me as I am, and you want to know how I really am. You're my friend, and I feel I can tell you when I'm low, what's bothering me, and where it hurts. And I'm so grateful when you call and ask, 'And how are you, Helen?'"

Candor

Candor is not an obvious quality of gracious care-receiving, but as a number of stories in this chapter indicate, it is an asset when the relationship to the caregiver is open and secure. Candor is not an asset when it's likely to engender defensiveness and certainly not when it is an instrument of hostility or disdain. It is only an asset when the care receiver trusts that her openness will strengthen the relationship on which she depends and encourages the same kind of candor on the part of her caregiver.

Characteristics of Caregivers That Elicit Gracious Care-Receiving

This book is about receiving care. It shares the shortcoming of books on caregiving in its narrow focus on one side of a mutual relationship of giving and receiving. A brief shift in focus to caregiving will not eliminate the imbalance, but it will serve to show how intertwined are the gracious giving and receiving of care.

Three characteristics of gracious caregivers deserve special mention:

- Faithful presence
- Empathic listening
- Respect

By **faithful presence** I mean quite simply being there on a regular basis and open to the unfolding of the moment—no small thing in the lives of busy caregivers with heavy demands on their time. I am thinking particularly of the "sandwich generation," parents (usually mothers) who provide care for their children and their parents. The faithful ones find the time to show up, to be there, often at great personal cost. There is, of course, a difference between showing up and being there, being present. But you can't be a faithful presence if you don't show up in the first place. There are some who "show up" out of a sense of duty, with barely concealed resentment that keeps them from being fully present, but most are there because they want to be. That and that alone is all that is needed to be fully present, and that is enough to elicit gracious receiving.

A good friend and colleague from Valparaiso, who is a model of faithful presence, told me about giving care to his father in the last few weeks of his life and how that experience helped him overcome his resistance to receiving. He states: "I'm ashamed to admit how often I've thought that I'd sooner do away with myself than to become totally dependent. And yet, when I had the opportunity to care for my father when he was in home hospice care for the last month of his life, I experienced some of the most difficult but also the richest moments of my life by having the opportunity to care for him."

The colleague, an Old Testament scholar, noted that the Hebrew of the commandment to honor parents has to do with accounting for the heaviness of a parent; that is, for the weight of their love for us, and especially the love of which we can't even be aware. "While impersonating a hospice nurse and caring for my father, I came to see that honoring parents also includes the opportunity to return that love, in my case long after my comatose father was no longer aware he was loved and being cared for. After that experience, I hope with all my heart that I am a big enough person to receive care gracefully some day myself if circumstances should make that necessary or inevitable."

Another example of faithful presence was when our firstborn was hospitalized at age nine months with double pneumonia and not expected to live through the night. Our pastor came to the hospital. He sat with us for at least two hours and didn't say more than five sentences the whole time. If he had said much more, I would have kicked him out. We were in no mood for conversation or pious platitudes. But he was there and shared our agony. That always comes to my mind when I think about the meaning of faithful presence.

I need not cite more examples. I'm sure you could easily call to mind a dozen or more from your own experience. The people who possess the quality of faithful presence are usually quiet, unassuming, and empathic. They are angels of mercy and usually received as such.

Empathic listening means attentiveness to both the verbal and nonverbal expressions of need from the person receiving care. As a broad generalization, some people are talkers and some are listeners, and it's not hard to tell the difference at a meeting or social gathering. Listeners, however, are not necessarily empathic. Indeed, they may be highly critical of the person who is talking, either one-to-one or in a group, which is the opposite of empathic. Or they may be just bored or listless.

An empathic listener understands the person she is with in the sense of "standing under" where he is standing and seeing and feeling what he is seeing and feeling. She is in tune with nonverbal communication, such as facial expression, body posture, and tone of voice. Some people have a natural gift for empathic listening, others can benefit from training. Pastors, counselors, Stephen Ministers, and those in other kinds of caring ministries are trained in the art of listening to enable them to better discern the needs of those whom they care for.

Empathic listening elicits expressions of need and an openness to receiving care. Willingness to listen can be signaled by how you greet people, especially those who are needy. There is a big difference between "How ya doin'?" and "How are you, really?" The latter is an invitation to receive care, an invitation that is confirmed by empathic listening.

Faithful presence and empathic listening, as well as other qualities of gracious care-giving, have received ample attention in the extensive literature on providing care. The quality of **respect,** however, is not prominent in the literature. A caregiver may behave in a kind and thoughtful manner but lack respect for the person receiving care. Mutual respect is a given in relationships of equals, but is often lacking when all the power and honor in the relationship belong to the person giving care. Thus the caregiver may develop an exaggerated sense of self-importance, and the care receiver a diminished sense of self-respect.

I learned the importance of respect from a former student at Valparaiso University. She appeared one evening at the Chapel Counseling Center without an appointment. Unable to speak and shaking with fear, she had the highest level of anxiety I have ever encountered in a person who was not hospitalized. That night marked the beginning of a counseling relationship that continued throughout her college years and beyond.

From a deeply needy and vulnerable infant in her regressed state, she gradually grew into an emotionally mature and exceptionally caring person. I asked her, as I did many others, to share with me her experience of receiving care. She commented particularly on the importance of mutual respect:

> You always showed me deep respect—by paying such careful attention to me, by seeing and celebrating my strengths, by being open to the ways in which I could give something to you, such as teaching you something or acknowledging what you went through to care for me. In a way appropriate to a parent-child relationship, the giving was *much* more heavily in the you-to-me direction for many years—but still, part of your respect for me was acknowledging that I also gave to you. You did not *ever* convey the impression that you wanted me to stay dependent or needy, or that you wanted to see me as *sick* in order that you might be on top as the *healthy one*, the *giver*. You always communicated both your recognition of the reality and goodness of my great need and your confident expectation that I would grow up and that my growing health and strength would be something to celebrate.

Respect is the difference between compassion and pity. Two people who are equally competent and faithful in the care they provide may approach their caring in quite different ways. One perceives herself as The Helper and has pity on The Needy One,

The Sick One. The other recognizes that the situation could be reversed, that both partners in this relationship are needy and that both are helpers. To pity is to define yourself as different from the person in need, while compassion declares your solidarity with the person in need. Pity is like charity without mutuality, without the possibility of the receiver giving in return.

When the Loving Caregiver Needs Care

Your husband has a stroke. Your mother has Parkinson's disease and has moved close by at your suggestion. You thought you'd have lots of time for leisure and travel when the kids left home. Instead you're spending most of your time, day in and day out, taking care of your husband and mother.

You're not alone. More than 15 million Americans care for family members, usually a spouse or an elderly parent, who are chronically ill or living with a handicap. You love your husband and mother and are eager to meet their every need, but gradually their care is draining all your energy. If you find yourself in this position, it's time for you to make some changes. The greater the demand on your time and energy as a caregiver, the more you need to pay attention to the care you need from yourself and others.

In a study of older caregivers caring for their spouses, those reporting mental or emotional strain due to their caregiving duties were more likely to die during the four-year study than were older adults who weren't in a caregiving role during the same period.

You are at greatest risk if you believe you're the only person who can provide the care needed by the person(s) you love. That's setting yourself up for disaster if you're in this for the long haul. There are other people who can and will help you face this challenge. Learn to say yes to their offers. Though you may feel self-conscious or even guilty in doing so, ask for help and counsel from your family, friends, and fellow church members.

You may be surprised by their response. Above all, do not make decisions for them. Respect their right and responsibility to decide for themselves.

For all the reasons noted in this chapter, asking for help does not come naturally or easily, especially for caregivers. The more invested one is in the role of caregiver, the more difficult it is to switch roles and become a care receiver. I have no evidence for this statement other than my personal experience and countless discussions with other caregivers. If accurate, these dedicated and often irreplaceable caregivers are at high risk if they do not pay closer attention to their own needs.

Be alert for signs that you need help, such as losing patience, lacking joy, finding it difficult to sleep, losing your appetite, and feeling despair. There are things you can do to care for yourself, such as taking a daily walk, getting a nap when you can, and going for that checkup you've been putting off. You can also look for ways to receive care. Get a massage. Take a friend out to lunch and talk about anything other than your life as a caregiver.

Check out services in your church or community that provide respite care so you can take a break from your role as caregiver and do things to replenish your spirit. If there is no such service, talk to your pastor or parish nurse about initiating one. The parish nurse in our church did so, and it is one of the most valuable services our congregation provides.

Once you shift your attention to your own need of care, lots of ideas will occur to you beyond the meager suggestions I've made. It's the shift of awareness from yourself as caregiver to your own need of care that is the first and most important step. Unfortunately, you won't get much help in making that shift from sermons in church, feature stories in the media, or even Scripture, all of which praise the virtues of giving care. It's high time for us to embrace the need and the goodness of receiving care, especially for those who are overwhelmed by the caregiving they provide.

Conclusion

The epigraph to this chapter appears to be in direct contradiction to the one in the previous chapter. Is it better to give than receive? St. Paul, quoting Jesus, says that in regard to helping the weak, it is. Abba James says the opposite in regard to hospitality. Both statements are true, depending on the context and the emphasis. Missing from both statements is an appreciation of the mutuality of giving and receiving, each an essential good in every relationship.

There can be no genuine mutuality of giving and receiving unless both parties in the relationship can receive graciously, which makes this chapter almost as important for those who give care as it is for those who receive it. The substance of this book, both the theory and the practice, ought to be included in every course on pastoral care, every training program for Stephen Ministers, and in every sermon, essay, and book on meeting the needs of others.

It's the vulnerable and needy who have been on my mind throughout this writing project. That includes all of us all the time, though we are likely to be fully aware of it only at some points in our life. To those who are aware of their vulnerability and neediness, I say wholeheartedly with Abba James, "It is better to receive hospitality than to offer it."

The stories in this chapter reveal why it is so difficult to receive hospitality and why so many of us need to learn this practice of faith so that we may grow in the grace of receiving. Those who acknowledge that they are needy and vulnerable are our teachers in the art of receiving care in the same way that the dying are our teachers in the art of dying. We die as we live. If we have not learned the art of receiving care by the time of our dying, we are more likely to die alone, fighting for control, and resisting the efforts of those who would help when we most urgently need their help. From that, good Lord, deliver us.

chapter four

GIVING AND RECEIVING IN SOCIAL ENCOUNTERS

He is a good man, who can receive a gift well.
—Ralph Waldo Emerson

There are social norms in all cultures that govern behavior in relationships of giving and receiving. The strength of the literature on social exchange theory, fairly extensive but limited in scope, is the information it provides for understanding the social norms that are a powerful influence in shaping behavior in this society, including, of course, social exchange among Christians.

As previously noted, the pastoral care literature is devoted almost exclusively to giving care to those in need. Missing is a strong emphasis found within the social science literature on the reciprocity of giving and receiving. A review of this literature raises a central question for the church's ministry to those in need of care. If healthy relationships are reciprocal, should we not pay closer attention to the dynamics of exchange between those who give care and those who receive it? When someone responds to my need, I can reject the care that is offered, accept it grudgingly, or receive it graciously. So also with providing care, which can be given incompetently, done grudgingly, or offered graciously. The dynamics of the exchange are complicated and varied, and the research done on social exchange is a helpful reminder that neither receiving nor giving care can be properly understood apart from the mutuality of relationships.

For all of its emphasis on reciprocity, social exchange theory is also weighted on the side of giving help. Only a few studies focus on the person who receives help. The factors that determine if and when people will help the less fortunate are fairly well defined, but much less is known about the psychological conditions that lead people to seek needed help or the variables that affect how the recipient reacts to receiving aid. Since public and private agencies in the United States apportion billions of dollars each year to international, national, and local aid, it is surprising that so little research attention has been directed to the effect of aid on the recipient's feelings and perceptions.

Social Rules Governing the Giving and Receiving of Care

The reciprocal relationship between giving and receiving can be satisfactorily maintained only when the exchange is acceptable to both sides. That can be accomplished with relative ease in work-related relationships, where "an honest day's wage is given for an honest day's work." Determining the exchange between giving and receiving in intimate relationships is much more complex. Rules governing such relationships are generally based on equity, equality, or need:

• Those concerned with **equity** strive to balance what is given with what is received. Most marriage partners strive for an equitable balance between giving and receiving with exceptions for such things as illness. Many studies show that an equity norm in intimate relationships is associated with satisfaction, commitment, and stability in these relationships.

• There are times when an **equal** division of resources is the rule, no matter how much each has contributed. For example, two people may share equally in payment of a restaurant bill even though the food ordered by one of the two was more costly. This happens regularly with friends and business associates.

• A **need-based** rule is in effect when benefits are given in response to needs. Parenting relationships are an example, but so also are relationships between partners where one is handicapped or chronically ill.

Margaret Clark, a leading social exchange theorist, makes a useful distinction between reciprocity in exchange relationships and reciprocity in communal relationships. Rules of equity and equality are operative in exchange relationships, where negotiations concerning benefits given and received conclude in a business contract. In communal relationships, each person is motivated to help the other when a need is evident. For example, a nurse comes home from work, where she is paid, to care for an ailing child with no expectation of a reward other than the return of the child's health.

At times the distinction between exchange and communal relationships is difficult to make. Is the relationship between pastor and parishioner an exchange or a communal relationship? Pastors are under contract to provide ministerial services to the members of their congregations. They are obligated to give care but expected to do so out of concern for the person in need without receiving a specific benefit in return. All congregational relationships are communal in this sense, but only members of the staff are paid for their ministry. Congregations take advantage of the communal relationship between pastor and congregation when they expect their pastors to work long hours for low pay out of concern for others and a commitment to serve.

The application of need-based rules will vary in different circumstances. One variable is the strength of the relationship. The stronger the relationship, the more obligated one feels to meet the needs of the other. One may have a communal relationship with a congregational member, one's best friend, and one's child. The child's needs take precedence over the friend's needs, which will likely take precedence over the needs of a fellow parishioner.

The most rigorous test of the communal ideal in a caring relationship occurs when one of the parties is very needy—emotionally, physically, socially, or spiritually. How long and under what conditions can one remain responsive to the other's needs in such a relationship? The same question can be asked from the perspective of the person receiving care. How long and under what conditions can a very needy person ask for help and receive it graciously?

When needs are great, an exchange relationship is usually more easily managed and less stressful than a communal relationship. A contract is established between a visiting nurse and the person she visits for a specified fee for services rendered. Both the giver and receiver of care know the terms of the contract and can change them or terminate the relationship. It is easier to ask for help in an exchange relationship and have legitimate expectations that the need will be met.

A communal relationship is much more complicated. As the needs of one party in the relationship become disproportionate to the needs of the other, equity will inevitably be compromised. The needs of the caregiver are often unmet or undermet if she or he is overwhelmed by the needs of the other party in the relationship. This can be managed in most cases quite well if the time period is limited, as, for example, when a spouse is critically ill or someone is grieving a major loss. In fact, a communal relationship can be deepened and strengthened by such an experience. But if a critical illness becomes a chronic condition, both the giver and receiver of care are likely to find themselves in troubled waters and unsure of how to manage the relationship without destroying the intimacy they both treasure.

Accepting help when there is little to offer in exchange

As Wendy Lustbader notes, accepting help is more complicated in communal relationships in which you "are subjected to other people's timing, to what helpers choose to give, and to the rhythms they impose." A 78-year-old homebound woman describes her feelings as she waited for her daughter to take her grocery shopping: "If she says she'll take me shopping sometime on Saturday, I get dressed early and go sit by the window. I like to be ready when she pulls into the driveway. I'm afraid to start on anything, because she could come any minute. If she doesn't come until two or three in the afternoon, I end up wasting a whole day waiting for her. I get mad at her, but I shouldn't. After all, she's doing me a favor. I have all day, and she's got to fit me into everything else in her life."

The frustration of fitting into someone else's schedule is but one of many impediments in receiving help graciously. Another is the inability to repay the helper. We can freely receive gifts of food from friends and neighbors at a time of need if we anticipate being able to do the same for them or others in the future. Studies consistently show that persons are reluctant to ask for or accept help when there is no opportunity to return it.

The implications for congregational helping ministries are clear. Parishioners are hesitant to accept care from Stephen Ministers. It is part of a pastor's function to give care to the sick. Family members can be expected to respond to the needs of each other as a familial responsibility. Stephen Ministers, on the other hand, care for fellow parish members voluntarily and without pay. This makes it harder for many people to accept help from them without feeling a sense of obligation to return the favor.

Mutual sensitivity to needs in a caring relationship

"Relation is reciprocity," Martin Buber said in *I and Thou,* his classic book on being in relation. There is give and take in every relationship, beginning with infants who have a compelling capacity to please and evoke a loving response from their caretakers.

Though not always conscious of it, we expect something in return for the help we give. An occasional smile, a thank-you, perhaps only the perception that the receiver is content or appears to be growing stronger. The response may be ever so subtle, but some indication of gratitude or growth both satisfies the giver and enhances the mutuality of the relationship.

When working in concert, those who give and receive help are like dance partners who anticipate the movement of the other and respond in kind. A person who receives graciously can relax into the rhythm of the relationship and use freedom, creativity, and spontaneity to enrich the reciprocal relationship. In like manner, a perfunctory thank-you spoken with no emotion in either voice or facial expression can easily prompt the helper to respond in a similar manner.

It is in the self-interest of a care receiver to act in a manner that will encourage continued care, and the stakes are high in a long-term dependent relationship. A good care receiver is adept at sensing what his caretaker needs to make the relationship reciprocal. However, the burden of adapting to the other in a caring relationship ought not rest solely with the person receiving care, though he may feel that way because of his need to do something, anything, for a loved one who is providing extraordinary care.

The ideal relationship is mutual sensitivity to needs. A sensitive caregiver will pay close attention to subtle expressions of feeling, anticipate unasked questions, and be alert to confusion about the challenges that lie ahead. A sensitive care receiver learns when it's best to ask for help and when to say thank you or tone down expressions of thanks.

Mutual sensitivity is possible only where there is mutual trust between giver and receiver. An infant learns to trust the loving care of her mother before she has any awareness of or sensitivity to all that is required to provide that care. As the infant grows, mutual trust develops between mother and child. In a trusting relationship, the child will in time become sensitive to her mother's needs as she develops the capacity to see the world from her mother's perspective. Only trust and sensitivity can sustain relationships of giving and receiving care throughout life.

When the trust level is high, there can be complete honesty in discussing care issues without the fear that it will undermine the relationship. A care receiver who trusts that the person providing care will not use her power against him will more likely be sensitive to her needs. A caregiver who trusts that the person receiving care will not use his condition to manipulate her will more likely be sensitive to his needs. Mutual trust takes time to develop and though it is never achieved perfectly, the success of the relationship depends on its presence.

As noted in the previous chapter, mutual sensitivity to needs is enhanced by mutual respect. Respect for the caregiver is expected by both parties in a caring relationship. In addition, it is in the self-interest of care receivers to show respect even if they don't feel it. Respect for the care receiver, however, may be overlooked. Some of the worst examples I've seen are in extended-care facilities where men and women of great distinction are treated in demeaning and condescending ways because they are no longer self-sufficient and able to think clearly. Moreover, receiving care erodes self-respect because the skills of earlier years have vanished and independence has been lost. Under these circumstances, care receivers are apt to feel worthless. Caregivers need to be sensitive to diminishing self-respect and ways they might be contributing to it.

If each person is not sensitive to the needs of the other, a reciprocal relationship is not possible, as this report by an elderly woman demonstrates: "My son says he likes fixing me dinner every night, but he looks so tense when he's here. He comes over right from work, and his wife holds dinner at their house until he gets home. He smiles, makes chitchat, but I know he's racing against time. Sometimes he looks like he's going to explode, his face is so tight, but he keeps on smiling. I wish he could just say it's too much for him. I'd be disappointed, don't get me wrong, but microwave dinners wouldn't kill me." She is sensitive to her son's needs. Despite the sacrifices he is making in fixing dinner, the son is not.

Responding appropriately is a challenge for the care receiver because of ambivalent feelings about receiving care—feelings of gratitude in tension with feelings of resentment about dependency and loss of control. The challenge is what to do with the resentment, since most care receivers are rightly concerned that the expression of negative feelings may erode the social capital needed for the long haul in maintaining this much-needed relationship.

Make a Helping Relationship More Reciprocal

The terms *reciprocity* and *mutuality* do not pop up often in manuals, books, and essays on providing care, and when they do it's toward the end of providing better care. Thus caregivers are taught the art of listening, not because both partners must listen for any relationship to be mutual, but because listening will make them better caregivers. To offset that imbalance, let's focus on the receiver and how he or she can make a helping relationship more reciprocal.

Responding with gratitude for what is received

"Please" and "thank you" help smooth everyday life and are often most obvious in their absence. These ritual responses to even the smallest act of kindness, like holding the door open, are among the first that parents teach children, and however perfunctory, they are part of the social glue that helps maintain a civil society.

Saying thank you is particularly important in a reciprocal helping relationship. An unmet expectation of gratitude for even the slightest kindness, like a courtesy wave from the driver you've made room for in a line of traffic, can bring disappointment and even resentment. How much more so in a caregiving relationship. "What seems to be owed is 'sincere display,' a nod of the head, an open smile, a slightly sustained gaze. ... Payment is made in facial expression, choice of words, and tone of voice."

The setting in which one gives and receives help is a strong determining factor in how the help is received. Gratitude will come more naturally if the receiver is treated with respect, but one must be in a *position* to be treated thus. Recipients of food in a soup kitchen will likely find themselves in a setting that fairly shouts their status as "poor and needy." They gather outside until the doors are opened and then stand in line to receive a predetermined amount of food. How can you be grateful when there is a complete lack of mutuality between those feeding and those being fed? Contrast that with the intimacy of an infant suckling her mother's breast, where each is receiving from the other.

Maintaining autonomy in a helping relationship

The autonomy of caregivers is obvious. They can always walk away, even if there are enormous social pressures to remain in the relationship. Not so the receivers of care, whose heavy dependence erodes their autonomy, but it does not leave them without choices. They can in some circumstances terminate an unsatisfactory relationship or make it so miserable for the caregiver that the relationship is eventually badly crippled or completely destroyed. Such behavior may appear to be self-defeating, but so is a passive dependency that erodes self-worth, autonomy, and hope for the future. Hostile behavior toward one's caregiver may seem like the only power that remains in an ever-diminishing world.

However strong the feelings of hostility toward a caregiver, receivers need to be aware that such behavior is a destructive expression of autonomy. Noted social scientist Richard Schmitt suggests how a person with self-confidence and self-esteem can maintain a healthy expression of autonomy in a dependent relationship:

> It is true that autonomy includes a certain independence, but does it not also include the ability to ask for help when necessary and the ability to accept help gladly? Is it not precisely a mark of the autonomous person not to fear a loss of self at the slightest hint of dependence? Being able to ask for and accept help and still remain oneself requires autonomy of a much sturdier sort than that which cannot bear to acknowledge dependencies. (From *Beyond Separateness: the Social Nature of Human Beings—Their Autonomy, Knowledge, and Power.*)

The level of need in both parties will vary from one caring relationship to another, but if both partners in a relationship are autonomous, there can be full reciprocity and interdependence, even when the burden of care is heavily one-sided. As Schmitt notes, we can "distinguish between dependencies that are fruitful, which promote growth and enrichment and empowerment, and dependencies that are restrictive, which impoverish and stunt persons."

Managing the Feelings and Attitudes Engendered by Receiving Help

Managing attitudes and feelings, like resentment, is also a difficult challenge for both participants in a helping relationship, but especially so for care receivers. Caregivers are trained to deal with this challenge, but not care receivers, who have more to lose if they don't handle negative feelings well. On one occasion I was irritated with my oncologist, with whom I have an excellent relationship, because I was unable to reach him to discuss the findings of an MRI that would likely call for a major treatment decision. My inclination was to send him an angry e-mail message expressing my disappointment that he had not responded to numerous messages by phone and e-mail, but after some reflection I chose another way to deal with the situation, which I will reveal in a subsequent paragraph.

When there is inconsistency between the situation (being cared for), the conventional frame of reference (should be grateful and accommodating), and how we really feel (resentful), the options are to change the situation, change the frame of reference, or change the feeling.

To use the above example, changing oncologists was not a viable option for me. The dilemma was tension between the conventional frame of reference (be accommodating because doctors are busy people) and my feeling of irritation at not being able to contact my oncologist. So what to do? Using an alternative frame of reference (mutual respect and accommodation), I sent this message: "I assume there is good reason why I have not yet heard from you, but I want you to know that my life is virtually on hold until I know what lies ahead of me in the next weeks and months." We met in his office the day after he received this message.

A further analysis of this dilemma and suggested exercises for managing how we feel and think about our situation as care receivers are contained in Chapter 6 on "Workshops on the Practice of Receiving Care."

Differences in Gender, Age, Socioeconomic Status in Asking for Help

Everybody needs help all of the time. However, there are many, many variables that determine when and how often we are likely to seek help. We are fortunate to have a reliable body of scientific studies that identify the predetermining factors leading to a needy person's willingness to ask for help or respond positively to offers of help.

Gender. It will come as no surprise that females seek more help than males, at the rate of two to one. There are more female callers to radio counseling programs, more female clients of counseling centers, and more girls than boys who seek help in the classroom. A number of studies indicate that both males and females prefer seeking help from same-sex helpers, but this may be because the young adults studied (mostly college students) are likely to have closer friends of the same sex. This pattern remains the same for women who are married, but not for men. Married females rely on friends for help, but males are more likely to turn to their wives.

Females are more likely to seek help for problems of a personal/emotional nature, while males have a preference for instrumental/informational help. This is true also of male children, probably because the masculine sex role emphasizes goal achievement. Older social stereotypes depict males as strong and independent and females as weak and dependent. Nowhere is that more obvious than in older films and TV dramas. Males consistently rescue females from difficulty after plaintive pleas for help. Fortunately, the stereotype is fading with increasing portrayals of strong women in leading roles.

Age. A number of studies indicate that older adults tend to cope with problems by relying on themselves rather than by seeking outside help. The proportion of troubled individuals who seek help drops markedly after age 60. A likely explanation is the importance older persons attach to personal independence. Loss of independence leads to loss of control in older age. The psychological costs of requesting help are high if it means losing independence and control.

Socioeconomic status. There is a correlation between socioeconomic status and the kind of help one seeks. The lower on the socioeconomic scale, the more likely will a person look to others for the solution to problems. Those with a higher socioeconomic status are more likely to seek help in carrying out a task for which they are responsible. They make more requests for help, but in each such encounter seek less help than those with a lower socioeconomic status.

Personality differences among those asking for help

Self-esteem. Studies show that individuals high in self-esteem seek less help than those low in self-esteem. Low self-esteem employees seek more job-related advice. Women with lower self-acceptance scores are more willing to join women's counseling groups. This suggests that people with low self-esteem either have a greater need for help or are more willing to seek help. Those with high self-esteem regard help-seeking as inconsistent with their positive self-image. This is particularly true when the helper is a peer who may be rival for promotion or when there is no perceived opportunity to reciprocate. Those with scores high in self-esteem perform tasks that require reliance on the assistance of others less well than those whose self-esteem is not adversely affected by asking for the help they need. However, those with low self-esteem may overutilize helping sources because they perceive themselves as more dependent and are less confident in their own resources.

Achievement motivation. Because task completion is more important for high than low achievers, high achievers are more willing to seek help. This is moderated by the importance of the task to be completed. High achievers seek help when the ego-threatening aspects of help-seeking are minimal and perceptions of control are high.

Shyness. Shy students are less likely than students who are not shy to approach advisers with a request for help. This is the most pronounced when the helper is of the opposite sex. Avoiding interpersonal contacts may motivate the shy person to invest more in self-help efforts. Because shyness is a relational problem, an impersonal source of help, such as a computer, may be preferred.

Conclusion

Social science literature, though limited in scope, is the only available information on giving and receiving based on research studies. Though emphasizing reciprocity, the research focuses more on giving than receiving help. Perhaps that's because those doing the research think their findings are most likely to be useful to professionals in helping relationships.

Nevertheless, the research does provide valuable information about the dynamics of giving and receiving, information that can serve as a corrective to the generalizations we so easily make based on our limited experiences. This is not to negate the value of insight that comes only through personal experience, both our own and that of others. Stories like those in the Chapter 3 add depth and richness to the abstract and impersonal research findings in the social sciences.

part two

LEARNING THE PRACTICE
OF RECEIVING CARE

chapter five

PREACHING ABOUT RECEIVING CARE

Love cures people, the ones who receive love and
the ones who give it, too. —Karl Menninger

There is little about receiving care in the literature on pastoral care literature, and it is rare to hear a sermon on this topic. I've asked many pastors if they have ever preached a sermon on receiving care, and mostly I get a blank stare followed by a sheepish, "No, but I wish I had." Never has a preacher told me that receiving care would be an inappropriate theme for a sermon or even that the lectionary provided no occasion for it. The response has usually been something like: "I've never thought of that, but I think it's a great idea." My survey has been random, unsystematic, and limited, but I would be surprised if a well-designed poll resulted in a different finding.

This chapter contains selections from three sermons on the theme of receiving care, each with its own distinctive style. The first is a sermon I preached 15 years before my cancer diagnosis on the parable of the good Samaritan. Its focus is on the man who was beaten and in need of care. The second sermon, by Elaine Ramshaw on the parable of the friend who asks for help at midnight, is about the goodness of beseeching. The third sermon, by Gerald Wunrow on a familiar passage from the Sermon on the Mount, calls attention to the close relationship between giving and receiving. You may want to contrast these three with selections from a 19th century sermon quoted in Chapter 2 on "A Theology of Receiving Care." That well-crafted sermon represents a more traditional approach to the relationship between giving and receiving in Christian understanding.

In Need of Care—Luke 10:25-37

Tom Droege

Just then, a lawyer stood up to test Jesus. "Teacher, he said, "what must I do to inherit eternal life?" He said to him, "What is written in the law? What do you read there?" He answered, "You shall love the Lord your God with all your heart, and with all your soul, and with all your strength, and with all your mind, and your neighbor as yourself." And he said to him, "You have given the right answer; do this, and you will live."

But wanting to justify himself, he asked Jesus, "And who is my neighbor?" Jesus replied, "A man was going down from Jerusalem to Jericho, and fell into the hands of robbers, who stripped him, beat him, and went away, leaving him half dead. Now by chance a priest was going down that road, and when he saw him, he passed by on the other side. So likewise a Levite, when he came to the place and saw him, passed by on the other side. But a Samaritan while traveling came near him; and when he saw him, he was moved with pity. He went to him and bandaged his wounds, having poured oil and wine on them. Then he put him on his own animal, brought him to an inn, and took care of him. The next day he took out two denarii, gave them to the innkeeper and said, 'Take care of him; and when I come back, I will repay you whatever you spend.' Which of these three, do you think, was a neighbor to the man who fell into the hands of the robbers." He said, "The one who showed him mercy." Jesus said to him, "Go and do likewise."

The parable of the good Samaritan is about caring for others. That's certainly the point of the parable. But we miss something if we focus exclusively on the positive example of caring (the Samaritan) and the negative examples of the priest and Levite, who clearly do not care. You don't have to be a math major, though, to realize that for every caregiver there has to be someone who is a care receiver. That's the man who is beaten and left half-dead. This morning I would like to draw your attention to that man and what it means to be cared for.

The hero of the story is obviously the Samaritan who knows how to be a neighbor, to be one who cares. If the parable were told today, the Samaritan would be a Palestinian, not the kind of person you would expect to befriend a Jew. The Samaritan sets the standard by which Jesus judges not only the lawyer who asks the question about his neighbor, but all of humanity. Dietrich Bonhoeffer put it well when he said that Jesus' question at the last judgment will not be "What do you know?"—and even less "Whom do you know?" or "Who knows you?" Rather, the question will be "Where is your brother? Where is your sister? Where are those who have a claim on your care?"

For perhaps the first time I'd like you to focus your attention on the person most often neglected in the parable: the man who lies by the road, beaten, helpless, and very, very needy. It's not surprising that this pathetic figure by the road gets ignored. There is little that would prompt us to identify with him and his need. For the next few moments, I want you to think about that man and about what it means to be on the receiving end of someone's care.

We get all kinds of encouragement to care for others. We get very little encouragement to learn how to receive care. Contrary to the popular belief that it is easier and more pleasurable to receive than it is to give, for most people it is incredibly difficult to be dependent on the care of others. Yet all of us know that we are, at the very least, interdependent, and that we are never more than a heartbeat away from a serious illness or handicap. What about those times when we're like the man on the road, when we hurt, when we are in need of help? Fortunately most of us rarely or never find ourselves as totally dependent and as obviously in need as the man in the parable, but that's part of the problem. Most of our wounds are well hidden. We've been taught to cover them up with a smiling face or a stiff upper lip. We are encouraged to identify with the strong, the successful, the winners. Men at least are taught that tears are a sign of weakness, to be shed, if at all, in private. We've been taught to solve our own problems and not to burden others with them, especially people who are busy and have more important things to do.

But nobody is a winner all of the time. Everybody falls down. Everybody gets hurt. Everybody needs to be cared for. Everybody is dependent. It's just that we get so little help in being that way gracefully, humanly, with dignity. All of us value our independence, and few adults would want to exchange it for the childhood years of dependence, but there is a little child in each of us that surfaces at times with a yearning for arms that will lift up and enfold and a voice that whispers, "It's all right."

How hard it is at times like that to reach out and cry for help, especially if you're a man. How degrading it seems to admit that we can't solve our problems by ourselves. How difficult it is to become a beggar when self-sufficiency has been our ideal. We are born to win, or so it seems, and any losses sustained along the way we are expected to nurse silently—and alone.

There is a destructive and distorted theology that informs that mentality. We can all say quite glibly that we live by grace and not by works, but the truth is that most of us live by a labor theory of values which says that you are what you produce, that your human worth is judged by your strength and your ability to care for yourself and others. That's what's behind the worthlessness that people feel when they are weak, when they are dependent, when they lose. What a commentary on us and our values when our sense of dignity—and even our sense of humanity—is dependent on our being successful and strong and able to care for others! No wonder it is hard for us to ask for and receive help from others; in so doing we affirm their humanity and negate our own.

Only the perspective of the gospel can reverse that mindset and enable us to receive grace with grace. The truth is that we are all beggars before God, all totally dependent on the gifts that he so freely bestows, gifts of life and love and mercy. That's as true when we are healthy as when we're sick; when we're strong as when we're weak; when we're caring for others as when we're being cared for. All that we have and all that we are, our very humanity, flows from God and is sustained by God. Our worth is dependent not on what we do but on who we are as children of God. Ours is an alien dignity that has its source in God and not in ourselves, and that's what makes a hopelessly retarded child worth as much as the most gifted genius on this planet. That's a humbling thought when we get too proud of our strength and self-sufficiency, but it's a comforting thought when we're not producing what we think we ought to, and when we are aware of reaching out for and hanging on to the help of others.

In the parable of the good Samaritan, Jesus is identified with the Samaritan, the one who does the caring. In the parable of the last judgment, recorded in Matthew 25, Jesus is identified with the one who is cared for, the one in prison, who is hungry and in need. We need to be reminded that Christ is present on both sides, that he is in the caring and in the being cared for.

Bonhoeffer put it powerfully when he said: "Men go to God when he is sore bestead, find him poor and scorned, without shelter or bread, whelmed under weight of the wicked, the weak, the dead: Christians stand by God in his hour of grieving."

It's obvious to us that Christ is in the caring, that he works in and through us when we care for others. It's not always obvious to us that Christ is present on the other side, in the being cared for. It's no disgrace to be in need or to receive the help that others offer. Our Lord knew what it was like to be weak and alone, to suffer, and to be in need of help from others. He cries out with us in our weakness and aloneness, and he reaches out to lift us up. There is no contradiction in that, because his presence encompasses all of life and penetrates deeply into every human event. Pray God give us the grace to be loved as well as to love, to receive as well as give, and in so doing to affirm the gifts of God, who enables us to give only because we have first received.

Needing Care—Luke 11:5-13
Elaine Julian Ramshaw

And he said to them, "Suppose one of you has a friend, and you go to him at midnight and say to him, 'Friend, lend me three loaves of bread; for a friend of mine has arrived, and I have nothing to set before him.' And he answers from within, 'Do not bother me; the door has already been locked, and my children are with me in bed; I cannot get up and give you anything.' I tell you, even though he will not get up and give him anything because he is his friend, at least because of his persistence he will get up and give him whatever he needs.

So I say to you, Ask, and it will be given you; search, and you will find; knock, and the door will be opened for you. For everyone who asks, receives, and everyone who searches finds, and for everyone who knocks, the door will be opened. Is there anyone among you who, if your child asks for a fish, will give a snake instead of a fish? Or if the child asks for an egg, will give a scorpion? If you then, who are evil, know how to give good gifts to your children, how much more will the heavenly Father give the Holy Spirit to those who ask him!

The parable of the friend at midnight is about the importance and power of asking. It's a picture of how asking can make a difference when nothing else will, of the power of God working in the world in the unlikely form of a supplicant who doesn't have a leg to stand on. As the reign of God is figured in the growth of a tiny seed into a large plant, or the working of a little bit of starter in a huge mound of flour, so, perhaps, it is figured in the persistent asking of someone who has no coercive power at all, only the power of need given voice. This may be a picture of God's power to change the world, power hidden in apparently powerless forms, power that doesn't look or operate at all as we would expect it to, as we often want it to when we pray.

God *does* respond to us out of connection to our need, out of loving relationship, as a father responds to the requests of the children he loves.

I can't think of God's response to our asking, our beseeching, without thinking of how Julian [of Norwich] depicts Christ's attitude toward our prayers. Here is part of what Julian says:

> Beseeching is a true, gracious, enduring will of the soul, united and joined to our Lord's will by the sweet, secret work of the Holy Spirit. Our Lord himself is the first receiver of our prayer, as I see it, and he accepts it most thankfully, and greatly rejoicing in it, he sends it up above and sets it in among his treasures, where it will never perish. It is there, before God with all his holy ones, continually being received and continually assisting our needs. And when we shall receive our bliss, our prayer will be given to us as a measure of joy, with his endless thanks so full of honor. Our Lord is full of gladness and delight at our prayers. He looks out for them,

for he wants them longingly. For by means of his grace they make us grow like himself in condition as we are in kind. ... Because of the reward and the endless thanks he wants to give us, he covets our continual prayer in his sight.

It may be hard for us to imagine the mutual joy in need that Julian describes. I think it's true that we all learned our own worth, if we learned it at all, when our need was welcomed, honored, by another, so that we could know our very asking to be good. But on a day-to-day basis, we are often conscious of experiencing others' need more as a burden or a drain than as a gift. And we certainly tend to think our need must be a burden to Jesus, even if he does self-sacrificially take that burden on.

Certainly the man with the bread being roused at midnight experiences the friend's need primarily as a burdensome demand. But that is related to the fact that he does not respond out of his friendship, out of a deep connection to the friend's need. And God always does respond to us out of loving relationship, like a loving parent. God's joy at our need is like the joy of a nursing mother gone too long between feedings, when her baby clamps its lips on her nipple and sucks. It is like the joy of a parent when a daughter who has almost died of anorexia comes one day to the dinner table hungry. It is like the joy of a woman whose husband, instead of walling himself off in his pain to keep control as masculinity demands, chooses this night to turn to her, to show her his grief and fear, to let her in. That, I think, is the joy that Julian had in mind, when she envisioned Jesus thanking us eternally for our prayers. The other's need is a gift, because we want so much to give, to connect, and we can't do that if they don't *ask*.

We can be sure that God loves our asking, welcomes our need, puts each prayer in her treasure house, and will thank us for it eternally. We can be sure that God, like a loving parent, wants to give us all good things and no evil thing. We can be sure that God does act in response to prayer: healing, freeing, changing the world, although the power of God doesn't look like we expect it to. Not like the might of kings and horses, but like mustard seeds or sourdough starter, or a persistent questioner in the night. We can be sure that when we pray for a good thing and evil nonetheless happens, we are not pushed outside the story of God's people. We can be sure that one day, as Julian put it, God will do some great thing, so that all will be well. That wasn't a statement for her about the way things will be for us today or tomorrow. It was an eschatological statement about what God would do at the end of time to set all right.

We can only pray as Christians in the shadow of the cross and in the light of Easter. We pray remembering that Jesus was not delivered from torture and death, and that God raised him up, not erasing the evil of his torture and execution, not erasing the evils of human history, but showing us a bit of God's future ahead of time, in the wounded hands of Jesus breaking for us the bread of heaven.

So pray for the bread you need today, and pray for God's kingdom to come, when the loaves will be multiplied to feed the whole world on the mountain of God. And come to this table, bringing all your need, that God might delight in it, and honor it, and thank us for coming.

Receiving Is the Other Side of Giving—Luke 6:38
Gerald Wunrow

Give, and it will be given to you. A good measure, pressed down, shaken together, running over, will be put into your lap; for the measure you give will be the measure you get back.

We're all aware that Jesus, while here on earth, went around "doing good." He instructed his disciples and other followers: "Do good unto all people and especially to those who are of the household of faith." As we become his followers, the command is directed to us, too; our very purpose in life is to "do good" to all, even to our enemies, "'as we have opportunity."

Sometimes, maybe even often, Christ's followers have lost sight of the fact that love, charity, and doing good must be a two-way street. That is, if we want people to feel comfortable when we share with them, we must be open and willing not only to give but also to receive in return from them and from others. That means we need to acknowledge that while we have strengths and gifts we can share with others, we also have weaknesses and needs, and we need help from God and from others.

That's what Jesus is saying in our text, "Give and it shall be given to you." It isn't that we earn the latter by doing the former. But that's just the way it is. Even when we feel very independent and self-sufficient, we still have dependency needs. And that's okay. That's how God made us. We all need to be givers and receivers. Because we all have gifts and we all have needs. To insist that I must always be the giver and the other person must always be the receiver is condescending and actually a kind of selfishness. Giving makes us feel good. That's okay. But the recipient needs to give too and feel good. That requires that others, including me, need to acknowledge that we need the gifts others have to give.

When that reciprocity is missing, little wonder that "doing good" and "charity" are resented. They are experienced as manipulation, control, and condescension. Is that why our national efforts to aid other countries are sometimes resented? Is that why our church's efforts in the inner city are sometimes rebuffed? Is that why children and teens especially resent us as parents and grandparents? We intend to give out of our gratitude for what God has given us in Christ, and our sincere compassion for others of his children who are in need. But instead we come across as feeling superior, wanting to feel good at the receiver's expense.

Often I've heard caregivers in our Stephen's Ministry say, "I think that I get more out of my visits than I give." I have often asked these caregivers, "Have you shared these feelings with your care receivers? They need to know that *you*, too, are receiving much from this relationship."

Jesus was a master at receiving as well as giving. As God, he was and is the greatest giver of all. Yet on many occasions he allowed, and even sought out, the gifts of others to meet his own needs. Remember when Jesus challenged his disciples with the problem of feeding the 5,000? A rather naive little boy stepped forward and offered his lunch. The disciples diminished and discouraged the offer. But Jesus blessed the gift and shared it with the others. I dare say that little boy never forgot that experience. I suspect it transformed his life. Or how about the time in the Garden of Gethsemane when Jesus unashamedly said to three of his most trusted followers, "Watch and pray with me, I need the strength and encouragement of your presence and of your faith in my hours of trial." Sadly, the disciples failed to take seriously Jesus' need. How much these "caregivers in training" missed that night and how much Jesus missed, too! There are many similar biblical examples of Jesus not only as willing to give care but also to receive it. What an example for us!

It was not only in Jesus' humanness that this was true. As God, he also comes to us and says, "Give and it will be given to you. You need the gifts I have to offer: grace, forgiveness, hope, purpose. But I also need your prayer, praise, and thanksgiving." Just think of it! God needs me! He says, "Whatsoever you do and share in love with even the least of human kind, you're doing and giving to me."

What a powerful example he sets for us! God is a giver and receiver in relation to us, and we are to be givers and receivers in relation to others. Children need parents and parents need children. The old need the young and the young need the old. The infirm need the healthy and the healthy need the infirm, the strong need the weak and the weak need the strong. We all are able and we all are dependent. We are *interdependent.*

How many times I've been at a death bed as grieving parents try to keep the children away—perhaps to protect them from sadness! Perhaps to protect themselves from the children's more honest expression of grief. But when the children are allowed to share in this great transitional moment of life, so often they end up comforting the adults by their questions, their tears, and their faith. We need each other! What a relief when we can share our moments of strength. But we can share our moments of weakness, too. We can share our independence, and we can share our dependence. We can share our health, but we can also share our vulnerability. We can share our faith, but we can share also our doubts.

Let me close with this final reminder: We've said that giving is a two-way street. In reality it is a three-way street. It all starts, of course, with God's initiative. "In this is love, not that we loved God but that he loved us and sent his Son to be the atoning sacrifice for our sin" (1 John 4:10). That's where the whole process really starts. In humble, penitent, and grateful faith we receive his forgiving and transforming love for us! Then, empowered by God's unconditional love for us, we reach out to share love with others. Yet in the process, we remain needful and vulnerably open to receive their gifts of love in return. And so the process continues. God to me, to others, back to me, and back to God. It is indeed the love that makes the world go round!

Conclusion

Though there has to be a care receiver for every caregiver, I'm not suggesting that an equal number of sermons should be preached on each. It is obvious that the overwhelming emphasis in Scripture is on giving care with Jesus as the supreme model. It's the almost total absence of any attention to receiving care that is the problem. Is it too much to suggest that at least one sermon a year be devoted to care-receiving? If not that, then at least a paragraph on care-receiving in every sermon on caregiving. The point here is not the number of sermons or references in sermons to care-receiving, but rather a pastoral awareness that people need encouragement and instruction in receiving care. When that is so, sensitivity to the needs of the care receiver will shape the content of almost every sermon.

chapter six

WORKSHOPS ON THE PRACTICE OF RECEIVING CARE

When practices are faithful, they teach us surprising things about God, our neighbors, and the world.
—Dorothy Bass and Craig Dykstra

The practice of faith is a better indicator of what people believe than the statements of faith they profess. That observation usually accompanies a charge of hypocrisy: "What you do speaks so loudly that I can't hear what you say."

But it's equally true that a genuine practice of faith lends credibility to one's profession of faith. The focus in this study is on the faith practice of receiving care, and this chapter is devoted to ways that people can deepen their experience of this practice.

Dorothy Bass, editor of *Practicing Our Faith,* writes: "We yearn for a richer and deeper understanding of what it means to live as Christians in a time when basic patterns of human relationship are changing all around us. ... Most of us continue to look for greater insight into how our faith can help us discern what we might do and who we might become." Each chapter of *Practicing Our Faith* focuses on a faith practice, such as honoring the body, hospitality, keeping Sabbath, forgiveness, healing, and dying well. As this book demonstrates in each of these chapters, weaving faith and practice into a seamless whole is the goal of Christian living.

Receiving care is a faith practice, as is giving care. Giving and receiving are not in themselves religious, but the practices of giving and receiving are informed by faith and reflect one's faith. Both practices need to be learned and practiced regularly. The church has given ample attention to the practice of giving care through sermons, workshops, manuals, and specialized ministry training in programs like Stephen Ministry and Befrienders. Little attention, however, has been given to the practice of receiving care. That imbalance is reflected in theological studies, pastoral care literature, and sermons.

Much-needed changes in understanding the need to receive care graciously can come through the preaching and teaching ministries of the church. That is not enough, however, for effecting behavioral change. Learning the faith practice of receiving care takes practice.

There are many ways to learn the practice of receiving care:

- A workshop of structured exercises to experience receiving care
- Support groups in which members both give and receive care
- The practice of guided imagery, in which the leader guides the participants in an experience of receiving care
- Rituals such as foot washing that are grounded in Scripture and church practices
- The practice of meditation, which can include the experience of receiving self-care

This chapter contains a series of workshops that include exercises for gaining practical experience in receiving care. They are designed to assist people in reflection on the care they are receiving now in interdependent relationships and the care they can anticipate receiving when they are more vulnerable and dependent.

The chapter concludes with guidelines for support groups to help members sort out the dynamics of receiving care. A set of guided imagery exercises on receiving care compose the major portion of Chapter 7, along with suggestions for incorporating self-care into the practice of meditation.

Workshops

Parish pastors, parish nurses, or Stephen Ministers are the congregational leaders most likely to lead workshops on receiving care, though anyone familiar with group process can serve in this capacity. A workshop can be held in any room large enough to allow free movement for those attending. Though not necessary, a congregational setting will enhance the faith dimension of receiving care: perhaps an adult forum, a training session for Stephen ministers, an open invitation to congregational members who recognize their difficulty in receiving care, or a special program for a particular group. Careful attention to the title of the workshop and how it is promoted will be crucial to its success. Suggested titles are provided, but workshop leaders are encouraged to use their imagination for the best possible title.

Since so little attention is given to the role of care receiver in our society, including the church, the promotion of workshops will be the greatest challenge of congregational leaders. Prior to the scheduling of one or more workshops, encourage Bible study groups, educational leaders, and pastors to introduce this topic whenever possible. For example, an adult class on the differences and similarities between receiving care from God and receiving care from family and friends will prompt members of the class to think about this topic in relation to their faith. An article in the congregational newsletter that draws from information in this book will likely stimulate interest in the topic. A sermon on care-receiving will also bring the topic to the attention of congregational members. Examples of such sermons can be found in Chapter 5.

Introductory Workshop #1
Sharing Experiences in Receiving Care

A workshop that not only draws on the experiences of those attending but also facilitates the sharing of such experiences with others is an excellent way to begin a series of sessions on receiving care. This workshop also works well as a stand-alone session that has the potential to evoke sufficient interest for additional sessions at a later time.

In this workshop, participants are asked to complete one or more survey forms that are designed to evoke memories of receiving care. Several survey forms are included in the appendix for the workshop leader to photocopy and use.

Approximate Time of the Workshop
60 minutes

Purpose of the Workshop
• To assist participants in reflecting on their experiences of receiving care
• To encourage participants to share with each other their experiences of receiving care

Process of the Workshop
Participants will fill out survey forms concerning their experiences of receiving care. They will then be divided into groups of up to four participants to share their responses to items on the survey forms.

Process of the Evaluation of the Workshop
Participants will be asked to record on blank sheets their reaction to participation in this exercise. Were they uncomfortable at any time? Do they have suggestions for additional items in the survey form? Would they recommend this workshop to others? Would they welcome the opportunity to participate in additional sessions on receiving care?

Instructions for the Workshop Facilitator
Introduce the workshop with some general comments on this topic. You might note how little attention has been given to it in the literature on care, including pastoral care. Thus a workshop on receiving rather than giving care is unusual, and they are to be complimented for their participation. Note also that as Christians we are reminded again and again that we are recipients of God's steadfast love and care, and we are encouraged to pray for help in time of need. Yet we often resist the care that fellow Christians offer in our time of need, and we are reluctant to ask for help. Assure participants that they are not alone if they feel uncomfortable about the prospect of receiving care, especially if it is over an extended period of time.

Begin the session with the suggestion that participants will learn more about receiving care from the collective wisdom of the group than from a presentation on the most effective ways to ask for and receive help from others. Distribute survey form (see appendix) along with pencils for those who need them. Urge the participants to take their time in filling out the form so that they can draw fully from memories of past experiences. One-word or one-sentence responses are not likely to be as helpful as more thoughtful reflections that include a reference to one or more experiences.

After participants have had sufficient time to complete the survey form, divide them into groups of two to four (if your group is large enough to divide) to share their experiences of receiving care. Since this will be the most interactive and informative portion of the session, allow adequate time (30 minutes) for a full discussion of shared experiences.

Reconvene the total group to identify common themes in the responses. Finally, distribute blank sheets of paper and ask the participants to write two or more ways in which they would like to improve their capacity to receive care, followed by a sentence or two on how they intend to accomplish it. (If the workshop group is too small for division, do the above concluding tasks with that group.) If more workshop sessions are planned, consider the option of setting aside time in a future session for a discussion on the progress they have made on their goals.

Introductory Workshop #2
Learning from Long-Term Recipients of Care

The very best teachers on the topic of receiving care are those whose physical condition (chronic illness, handicap) has placed them in a position of depending on others for daily care. The autobiographies of such people are useful sources of information about receiving care. Even more useful is the personal testimony of long-term care receivers, not only because personal witness is more credible and convincing than written stories, but also because it provides an opportunity for a question-and-answer session.

Title of Workshop
Learning from long-term recipients of care

Approximate Time of the Workshop
60 minutes

Purpose of the Workshop
- To better understand the challenges and opportunities of receiving care

- To benefit from the experience and wisdom of fellow Christians who have depended on others for care over extended periods of time because of their physical, emotional, or spiritual condition
- To compare personal experience with the experience of other participants and long-term recipients of care

Process of the Workshop

Participants will be assembled in a single group, preferably in a circle if the group is small enough, to hear from one or more long-term recipients of care. Then participants will be divided into smaller groups (no more than four per group) to share what they have learned and compare their experience with others.

Instructions for the Workshop Facilitator

Recruit one or more long-term recipients of care to share their experiences. Generally, people who have something special to offer because of an experience are willing and eager to share that experience with others who could benefit from what they have learned. This is especially true if there is a communal bond between the presenter and the participants. Thus every effort should be made to recruit someone from the household of faith and, if at all possible, from the congregation sponsoring the workshop. Don't overlook the possibility of bringing someone from an extended care facility. Because residents of such facilities are often not given the respect they deserve, this workshop provides an opportunity to be appreciated for the expertise they have gained. Of course, no one should be pressured into this role if they feel uncomfortable doing so.

It will be easier to recruit people for this assignment if they are not doing it alone. Having two or more long-term recipients of care adds diversity and lessens the feeling of any one person being on the spot. In addition, comments by one person on a panel will often trigger a response from another panel member who had a similar experience.

If the group is large and more than one person will be sharing an experience, arrange the chairs in rows. Prepare a set of questions to ask the care receivers, such as:

- Describe the kind of care you have been receiving. Who provides the care and how long have you been receiving such care?
- What have been the greatest challenges you have faced as a care receiver?
- What has been your best experience as a care receiver?
- Can you think of a person who is a good example of receiving care graciously?
- How might those attending this session best prepare themselves for the role of care receiver?

After the panel presentation and general discussion, divide the participants in groups of up to four people. Encourage them to share what they have learned and how that compares with their own experiences. Avoid the temptation to include a long-term recipient of care in each group. Though the group will continue to learn from those participants' experiences, they are less likely to share their own feelings and attitudes about being a care receiver.

If the initial group is smaller and there is only one presenter, arrange the chairs in a circle and conduct an interview with the same type of questions as those above. After the interview and discussion, invite the participants to talk with the person(s) next to them in order to share what they have learned.

Learning to Receive Care:
A workshop with five sessions

A workshop with exercises in receiving care will be more meaningful and useful if preceded by one or both of the introductory workshops. The purpose of those workshops is to increase awareness of the role of care receiver and the need for better preparation to assume that role for short or long periods of time. The purpose of this five-session workshop is to provide training in the practice of receiving care. Each of the sessions contains exercises for learning the practice of receiving care.

Workshop Sessions

Session 1:	Exercises in Receiving Care
Session 2:	Breath Awareness and Guided Imagery
Sessions 3 & 4:	Managing Emotions and Feelings in Receiving Care
Session 5:	Asking for Help

Goals of Workshop

- To provide the opportunity for participants to experience care-receiving through non-threatening exercises
- To change the perceptions of participants who have negative feelings about receiving care
- To assist participants in finding a conceptual frame of reference that will enable them to move from negative to positive experiences of care-receiving
- To provide theological grounding for understanding care-receiving as a practice of faith

Session 1: Exercises in Receiving Care

Approximate Time of Session
60 minutes

Purpose of Session
To provide participants with the experience of receiving care

Process of Session
Three exercises of interactive engagement provide participants the opportunity to experience the interactive roles of caregiver and care receiver.

Process of the Evaluation of Session
Participants will be asked to share what they have learned and to comment on their comfort level during each of the exercises.

Instructions for Workshop Facilitator

Exercise 1 in Session 1
Form two large circles with those in the inner circle facing those in the outer circle. Taking turns, each participant will experience the role of receiver and giver. The giver takes the outstretched hands of the receiver and conveys her or his care through touch alone. No words are to be spoken by either person before or during the exercise. The focus of the exercise is on touch, so participants may choose to close their eyes in order to concentrate more fully on the sensation of touch. Rotate the outer circle by one and continue the exercise until participants return to their original position. Reverse the roles of receiver and giver and complete the circle once again.

Give participants the opportunity to share their experiences of the exercise. This can be done with the total group, but the best way to get everyone to share thoughts is to ask the original partners to share together. If some participants might be uncomfortable sharing, give them the option to pass.

Exercise 2 in Session 1

Using the same circle arrangement as before, have each person alternate between giving and receiving a handshake. The person giving the handshake initiates the exchange by extending her or his hand to the other person, who responds by extending his or her hand to receive the handshake.

Then ask them to make the handshake reciprocal. In a reciprocal handshake, both parties extend their hands simultaneously and attempt to convey both their giving and receiving greetings from the other party.

Instruct the group to remain silent during the exercise. Discuss the differences among the different handshakes and when each would be appropriate.

Members of the outer circle move to the next person. Repeat the exercise using the following variations so that each participant will experience the exercise and two variations.

A variant of the above exercise is giving, receiving, and resisting a hug. Discuss the nonverbal cues and ensuing dynamics for giving, receiving, and resisting a hug.

A second variant or additional exercise is to help participants sense the difference between objectively observing the other and subjectively responding to the presence of the other. Arrange the group as before but provide chairs so that pairs are seated and facing each other. One is designated as the observer and the other as the observed. The person being observed sits quietly as if posing for a portrait. The observers are told, "Look at your partner." After 15 seconds, they are told, "Now imagine your partner stretching out her or his hands to welcome you." Direct the partners to pay attention to the differences between the two ways of seeing the other person. Next, "Observe the face of your partner as if it were a portrait in a gallery." After 15 seconds, "Imagine that you turn away from the portrait and see the person in the portrait standing before you with hands outstretched."

What changes in your perception took place between observing your partner and experiencing his or her welcoming presence?" Next, have the observer and observed change positions. Invite the members of the group to share their experiences at the close of the exercise.

Exercise 3 in Session 1

Form groups of three. Designate one of the three as caregiver, the second as care receiver, and the third as participant observer. Before the beginning of the exercise, the person receiving care indicates why care is needed (bereavement, illness, loss of job, etc.), the occasion for the interaction (chance meeting, request for help), and who provides the care (family or friend, Stephen Minister, a stranger, a professional care giver). Role-play the interaction. At the close of the exercise, the participant observer comments on the care receiver's response to the care that is provided. All three discuss the interaction. Rotate until all three have played each role.

Session Two:
Breath Awareness and Guided Imagery

Approximate Time of Exercise
90 minutes

Purpose of Exercise
To provide a nonthreatening experience of receiving care

Process of Exercise
The workshop leader will guide participants in forming images of receiving care. Though all remain in the same room, there is no interaction with others during the exercise. A selection of guided imagery exercises is contained in Chapter 7.

Process of Evaluation

At the conclusion of the exercise, provide blank sheets of paper and ask participants to record their impressions. The comments should be anonymous to encourage complete honesty. As the exercise is discussed in the group, give participants the option to pass.

Instructions for the Workshop Facilitator

Exercise 1 in Session 2

Breath awareness is a good initial exercise in a session on guided imagery. Some participants may be aware of this practice, but it will likely be foreign to many within the group. Breath awareness is central to the Buddhist practice of meditation and is frequently used as an induction method in hypnosis and guided imagery. Though brief, this exercise can assist fuller participation in the guided imagery to follow.

The following quotation links breath awareness to receiving and would be a good way to introduce the exercise:

> Breath awareness teaches us the lessons of receiving, of letting go, and of the equality of receiving and letting go. Each inhalation is an act of receiving the simply given nature of life itself. The Christian mystic Meister Eckhart said, "For God to be is to give being. For us, to be is to receive being." Our very being is an act of receiving the act of being that God infinitely is. Each inhalation embodies this receiving perfectly. … Sitting still and straight in meditation, leaning into each inhalation with such childlike abandon as to wholly lose our balance in the mystery of receiving the miracle of our simply given life, we are awakened to God giving herself to us, in and as the inhalation that is being received. Wholly attentive to our simply given life we sit open to the realization that our very presence is an act of receiving the very Presence that God infinitely is. (From *The Contemplative Heart* by James Finley.)

After introducing the exercise by reading the above quote or saying something less abstract about the value of paying attention to breathing, invite the group to spend a few moments in breath awareness, silently saying "receiving" with each inhalation and "releasing" with each exhalation. Soft music, such as Pachelbel's *Canon in D,* will assist participants in relaxing and participating more fully in the exercise.

Exercise 2 in Session 2

Follow the exercise for breath awareness with a guided imagery exercise from Chapter 7. (Chapter 7 provides ample instruction on using breath awareness and guided imagery.)

Sessions Three and Four: Managing Emotions and Feelings in Receiving Care

Approximate Time of Each Session

60 minutes

Purpose of Sessions

To provide participants with a conceptual framework for understanding and managing their emotions and feelings, along with exercises to apply what they have learned to their own experiences

Process of Sessions

The third session begins with an interactive discussion of "feeling rules." If this discussion takes the full time allotted for this session, both exercises in this section can be scheduled for the fourth session. If time allows, one of the exercises can be included in session three and the other in the session four, preceded by a review of feeling rules.

Process of Evaluation of Sessions

At the end of each exercise, participants provide feedback on their understanding of "feeling rules" and the usefulness of these rules for assessing and altering their experience of receiving.

Instructions for the Workshop Facilitator
Interactive discussion on managing emotions and feelings in receiving care

Sessions 3 and 4 present a difficult challenge for a workshop leader in that participants must be familiar with the function of "feeling rules," which are social rules that determine appropriate ways to express feelings and attitudes. The most effective way to accomplish that is an interactive discussion of these social rules prior to engaging in an exercise that presumes an understanding of feeling rules. Participants will readily recognize these rules and how they shape behavior as the theory is explained, but they will not be familiar with the theory itself. The greatest temptation for a workshop leader is to hurry through an explanation of the theory without engaging participants in an interactive discussion that will enable them to apply the theory to their own behaviors. Allow sufficient time for such a discussion, and find ways, such as asking for examples, to encourage active participation.

There are three factors to consider in an attempt to lower resistance to care-receiving:

- The situation (being cared for)
- Conventional expectations for responding to the care received (gratitude)
- How one really feels (resentful, humiliated, indebted)

If you are in need of care, the situation obviously cannot be changed. The goal of a workshop on managing emotions is to help participants identify and resolve the tension between conventional expectations and their real feelings about the situation.

Ask participants if they are aware of such tension in their experiences of being cared for and, if so, how they usually resolve it. Many will likely say that they change their feelings or their attitudes to match what they think is expected of them, but they are not likely to know there are a variety of ways to do this.

In an essay published in *The American Journal of Sociology,* Arlie Hochshild describes a variety of techniques for altering emotions:

- Mental—changing ideas, images, or thoughts in order to change associated feelings; often called reframing
- Physical—changing negative emotions by breathing more slowly and by trying not to shake or look embarrassed
- Emotional expression—changing gestures in order to change inner feelings (trying to smile, cry)

Ask for examples of each of these techniques. A example of a mental technique might be, "I'm going to think of the person caring for me as an agent of God sent to make me whole." A physical technique example might be relaxing tense muscles and breathing more slowly. An emotional expression example might be remembering a happy event that evokes a smile. Examples can be personal, from observations of others, or purely fictional.

According to Hochshild, how one is expected to feel about situations like receiving care is dictated by social convention. The rules of feeling govern:

- Strength of feeling (from strong and passionate to moderate or weak)
- Content of feeling (grateful rather than resentful)
- Duration of feeling ("How may times do I have to say thank you?")

The expectation is that gratitude will be expressed for care received, even without a feeling of gratitude. Ask participants if they agree that this is a social convention and, if so, whether they think it's appropriate. Like other social conventions, rules about how you are supposed to feel can be obeyed half-heartedly or broken boldly, the latter with varying consequences. Social expectations will vary with the burden of caregiving. There is a big difference between the situation of a person who is totally dependent on the care of others and a situation where the care needed is minimal and time-limited.

Feeling rules in care giving/receiving relationships
The expectation of gratitude for small favors, such as holding the door open for the person following you, is easily met with a smile and a thank-you. When the burden of care is heavy, expectations are not so easy to meet. They vary with the situation. When care is provided for a fee, as would be the case with a visiting nurse, gratitude is appropriate but not obligatory. Social convention permits and even encourages the person receiving care to ask for help and protest if the request is not honored. When care is provided voluntarily, it is much more difficult to determine how one should feel. Gratitude is certainly expected, but how much and for how long? What if you don't feel grateful? Is it okay to ask for additional help if you already feel obligated?

Social expectations vary with gender. Men in our culture are expected to be strong, independent, able to handle their own problems, and unwilling to admit to weaknesses. Women, on the other hand, are expected to be in touch with their feelings, have a desire to please, and form close relationships. The implications for care-receiving are obvious. For example, when the feelings of a care receiver don't fit his self-understanding (such as believing that men don't cry or ask for help), he has to live with the tension, or change either his feelings or the way he views himself.

Ask participants if these generalizations are true to their experiences. Ask for comments about the difference between receiving care for a fee and receiving care from a family member or a friend. Ask for examples from their experiences when personal feelings and attitudes did not match social expectations in a particular situation. How did they resolve the tension between expectations and feelings?

To be in need of long-term care can be the impetus for a change in how one feels in a situation. Being stoic, independent, and self-sufficient (the prototypical strong man) prompts feelings and attitudes that are not useful for a person dependent on the care of others over long periods of time. The situation in which he finds himself may be a teachable moment, but it might also be too late if his feelings are so deeply embedded in a particular view of himself that to change threatens the very sense of who he is as a person.

One of the strongest arguments for a workshop on receiving care prior to the onset of a condition requiring long-term care is that it may enable participants to face this issue and make adjustments before they are confronted with the challenges of dependency and vulnerability. Because congregational members are not likely to feel the need for a workshop such as this, it will require vigorous leadership and aggressive promotion on the part of the pastor and health ministry team to draw attention to care-receiving workshops.

Another significant factor in managing feelings and attitudes has to do with *gestures* within social exchange that express what is owed another: gestures like greeting a caregiver (cool or warm), showing thanks (ritual, effusive, labored), and smiling (forced, expansive, warm, conventional). Ask participants for examples of tension between gestures that are expected by a caregiver and gestures that reflect the genuine feelings of a care receiver.

A care receiver might well agree that the expectation of gratitude for care received is fully appropriate, even if she does not genuinely feel grateful. She may display a superficial feeling of gratitude, though the feeling is not genuine. If the expectation of gratitude is deeply honored, the superficial feeling may become an expression of deep acting. "The most generous gesture of all is the act of successful self-persuasion, of genuine feeling and frame change, a deep acting that jells, that works, that in the end is not phony though it is none the less not a 'natural' gift."

Gestures become destructive when social conventions are ignored. For example, a care receiver jeopardizes the care he needs if he tries to control caregivers through obnoxious demands or uses gestures that belong in a different social exchange (such as flirting with his nurse).

Though the material on managing feelings and attitudes will likely jell with the experiences of those attending, do not assume that even a good interactive discussion ensures that participants understand how to manage feelings and attitudes and are prepared to apply that understanding to their own experiences. Unless one of the following exercises follows immediately after the discussion, review the materials covered with the aid of suggestions in the introduction to each exercise.

The purpose of the following exercises is to put people in touch with the feelings and attitudes they currently have toward receiving care and to explore strategies that might enable them to receive care more graciously.

Exercise 1 in Session 3 or 4

This exercise explores how participants cope when they feel resistance to receiving care that is freely offered. I've frequently heard Stephen Ministers say that congregational members rarely ask for their help and are slow to respond when it is offered. What feelings account for the resistance? What rules determine their feelings, and how were they learned? Which relationships seem appropriate for receiving care and which are likely to generate resistance?

Begin the session with a general discussion of feelings and attitudes that people have about receiving care. On a chalkboard or chart paper make a list of feelings and attitudes that are identified, such as shame and fear of dependence. Many people are not aware of descriptive words for their feelings and attitudes.

Be prepared to add words and phrases to the list that participants may not mention.

Provide a frame of reference for discussing these feelings by referring to the feeling rules discussed earlier. When the participants are ready to proceed, ask them to pair up with someone who is not a family member. Distribute copies of "Attitudes and Feelings When Receiving Care" (see appendix for this ready-to-photocopy sheet). Instruct the pairs to write a short response to these questions and then discuss them with each other.

An Alternative or Additional Exercise

Note: Exercise 3 in Session 1 is almost identical to the following exercise. The context in this session is different in that the focus is on the feelings of the care receiver.

Form groups of three. Designate one to be the caregiver, one the care receiver, and one a participant observer. The care receiver chooses one of the following situations (their situation may be either real or imaginary): loss of a family member, chronic illness, handicap, mental illness, divorce, or another situation in which care is needed. The care receiver then describes the situation in detail to the caregiver, who assumes the caregiving role appropriate to the situation, such as family member, friend, or parish nurse.

The exchange begins with the caregiver, who offers help in any way that he or she feels appropriate. The care receiver responds to the offer either normally or as he or she would like to respond in the future. Allow 5 to 10 minutes. The participant observer then shares his or her perceptions of the feelings expressed by the care receiver, including a sense of whether the care receiver was responding normally or as he or she desires to in the future. Follow with a discussion among the three about the exchange. Shift roles until all three have had the opportunity to fill each role.

Exercise 2 in Session 3 or 4

The purpose of this exercise is to examine how participants view themselves in situations where they are clearly in need of care and how that perception affects how they receive or ask for care. What is it within their self-concept that leads to either resistance or receptivity in receiving care? How does that differ in relationships with family, friends, and congregational members?

Begin the exercise with a general discussion of the types of self-understanding that people bring to receiving care. Suggest some obvious personality differences (independent/strong, dependent/weak; rational/objective, sensitive/thoughtful) and ask participants to suggest others. After a general discussion, ask each participant to jot down a brief description of his or her self-concept as a person in need of care. Following a brief exposition of the function of self-understanding in relation to feeling rules and social gestures, ask each person to pair up with someone who is not a family member. Distribute copies of "Self-Understanding and Self-concept in Receiving Care" (see appendix for this ready-to-photocopy sheet). Instruct the pairs to write a short response to the questions on the sheet and then discuss them with each other.

Additional or Alternative Exercises

• Ask participants to jot down on a piece of paper words or phrases that describe their self-concept, such as "never cry" or "in control." Divide participants into random groups of three or four. Ask each group member in turn to share a story about receiving care that reflects his or her self-understanding. Spend about 10 minutes on each person's story. The purpose of the exercise is to help participants understand how their self-concept was formed and how they would like to change it.

• Ask participants to share with each other how they would like to think and feel about receiving care. Either assemble those with similar goals in groups to plan strategies for achieving those goals, or make random assignments of participants to groups of three or four and ask group members to share with each other the kind of changes they would need to make in order to receive care or ask for help.

The challenge in this exercise is to examine the self-concept that individuals bring to care-receiving and reframe them in a manner that will enable participants to receive care more graciously. Rather than changing feelings or gestures to fit the self-concept, the purpose of this exercise is to reframe their self-understanding in a manner that is congruent with genuine feelings and gestures.

Session Five: Asking for Help
Group Sessions for Care Receivers and Their Caregivers

It is rare for care receivers and caregivers to have a frank discussion about the challenges that each faces in a relationship that is often difficult for both. In the healthiest of such relationships there is honest and open sharing about issues like dependency and control. In most cases, however, both parties shy away from sensitive issues. Care receivers are fearful of alienating those on whom they are dependent, and caregivers feel an obligation to be "nice" to someone who is needy and vulnerable. Thus negative feelings are buried and have destructive potential if they are not addressed.

Couple counseling is one way to address such issues, but that is not likely to happen until there are serious problems in the relationship triggered by heavy dependence of one upon the other. Troublesome issues can be addressed before they become divisive by scheduling group sessions for married couples or partners, though people may be reluctant to attend and will need time and encouragement before they are ready for open sharing on a sensitive subject.

Support groups that are already established offer an ideal format. There are support groups for people with a wide variety of illnesses (cancer, multiple sclerosis, Parkinson's), addictions, and handicaps. Most groups of this sort, including the one I attend for multiple myeloma, encourage caregivers to attend. Occasionally group facilitators are invited to our meeting to lead groups of care receivers and caregivers in sharing feelings about their respective roles.

Session for Care Receivers Only

From workshops I've conducted on care-receiving and from my own experience, I've gleaned a series of questions that care receivers wonder about but rarely have the courage to ask:

- Do you respect me?
- Will you help me choose what is best for me or are you going to use your power to control the relationship and determine what is best for me?
- Will you listen to me?
- Are you competent to provide the help I need?
- Will you keep what happens between us confidential?
- Can I trust you?
- Will you be honest with me?
- Can I count on you to stay with me no matter what?
- Can we work together?
- Will you be judgmental?
- What do you expect from me?

List the above questions on chart paper or a chalkboard and ask participants to add additional questions or comment on one of the listed questions. Encourage a general discussion about questions care receivers wonder about but are afraid to ask. Identify the questions that are of the greatest concern. Be sure the group addresses the issue of power, probably the most important issue and the most difficult to talk about. Identify the questions that are of the greatest concern. Ask for suggestions on how best to address the issue raised by the question. Encourage members of the group to talk about what keeps them from discussing these questions with their caregivers. Would they be willing to raise some of these questions in a counseling session or a joint meeting with their caregivers?

Session for Caregivers Only

The following questions that caregivers wonder about but rarely have the courage to ask come from my experience as a caregiver and suggestions from family members:

- What do you expect from me?
- Do you respect me as a competent and compassionate caregiver?
- Will you be honest with me? Will you accept my honesty?
- Will you be judgmental?
- Will you listen to me?
- Will we be able to work together as a team?
- Will you allow me, even encourage me, to express needs of my own?
- Will you honor the boundaries between us and allow me to set limits?
- Can I count on you to trust me to provide the best care I can?
- Can you trust me not to abuse the power I have in our relationship?

A session similar to the one for care receivers might begin by identifying additional questions that they are hesitant to ask. Identify the questions that are of the greatest concern. Ask for suggestions on how best to address the issue raised by the question. Be sure the group addresses the issue of power, probably the most important issue and the most difficult to talk about. Encourage members of the group to talk about what keeps them from discussing these questions with their care receivers. Would they be willing to raise some of these questions in a counseling session or a joint meeting with the person who is the recipient of their care?

To my knowledge, it is rare for a support group of both care-givers and care receivers to discuss relational issues when both are present. To overcome initial resistance to open sharing between those who give care and those who receive it, an initial session with separate groups is a good place to begin. After the two groups have met for at least 45 minutes, assemble the total support group and lead a general discussion of what both groups discussed.

If there is interest in the group to continue this process, arrange for a follow-up session so that individual care receivers and caregivers can be paired up to deal directly and openly with interpersonal issues. There should be no pressure to participate in such an exchange. A separate session will allow those who feel uncomfortable with the process to opt out. Introduce the session with a brief overview of the previous discussion. After 30 to 45 minutes of exchange between pairs of caregivers and care receivers, form groups of four or six to share with each other what they have learned through this process.

chapter seven

LEARNING THE PRACTICE OF RECEIVING CARE THROUGH IMAGERY AND MEDITATION

At the beginning of all action is an inner vision in which things to be are experienced as real.
—Abraham Joshua Heschel

Group interaction is a primary method for learning new skills in a workshop. For those not comfortable with group processes, learning can be impeded rather than enhanced in such a setting. Guided imagery is both personal and communal in that the private experience of most participants will be deepened in a group setting.

When you vividly imagine something, you are generating images that can be nearly as vivid as the actual experience. In your mind's eye, picture a bright yellow lemon in the your hand. Imagine taking a sharp knife in your other hand and cutting a wedge out of the lemon. As you take that wedge in your hand, notice how yellow the lemon is and how glistening drops of juice have formed on the edges of the fruit. Sniff its fragrance and then place the wedge in your mouth. Sink your teeth into its tender pulp. Experience the tartness as your mouth puckers up.

If you took the time to really imagine taking a bite out of a lemon, it's likely that the flow of saliva in your mouth increased and your lips puckered up. The imagery makes the experience real, as if it were actually happening.

That's an example of how you can be guided in the use of your imagination to experience something that you've done before, or that you can imagine doing now or in the future.

Guided imagery is a noninvasive way to deepen the experience of faith and faith practices. The use of imagery by Christians is a natural outgrowth of the rich use of images in Scripture, making it an appropriate tool for learning faith practices, in this case receiving care. It's unfortunate that the use of guided imagery by Christians has suffered the fate of guilt by association because of its use in New Age spirituality and the practices of some Eastern religions. I certainly share a concern about the content of such imagery and the uses to which it is put, but the *technique* of guided imagery is neutral. When the content of the imagery is Christian, as it is in parables and the stories and metaphors you hear in good sermons, it excites the imagination and enhances the experience and practice of faith.

Though guided imagery can be done as a solitary experience, my personal preference is a group setting because participants can more readily access their imagination if they follow the directions of a guide rather than serving as their own guides.

The guided imagery exercises in this chapter can be used as they are written or adapted for use by a workshop leader. It requires no training to use guided imagery for an individual or a group. If you are doing so for the first time, follow these simple rules to make effective use of this powerful tool to enhance the experience of care-receiving:

• Find a quiet place for doing these exercises and avoid interruptions as much as possible (cell phones and beepers, outside activity).

- Assure people in advance that they will remain in full control throughout the exercise. Guided imagery is not hypnosis.
- Never impose this practice on anyone. Honor the decision of those who choose not to participate.
- Speak slowly and with a calm, soothing voice to facilitate relaxation and access to the imagination.
- Prepare people in advance for silence. Many Americans are uncomfortable with silence, and it is important to explain its value: Silence allows an experience to unfold gradually. Allow ample time in the suggested periods of silence. Time will seem to pass more slowly for you than for participants in the exercise.
- You may want to use soft, soothing music in the background, such as Pachelbel's *Canon in D.* Avoid music that calls attention to itself.
- Ask for anonymous feedback on the value of the exercise to reassure yourself of the exercises' effectiveness, and as a guide to future use of this practice.

You will find a full description of the practice of guided imagery and step-by-step instructions for its use in the first chapter of *The Healing Presence,* a book of spiritual exercises on healing and wellness, published by The Youth & Family Institute.

Exercise in Receiving Care

Introduction

For group members who are unfamiliar with guided imagery, the leader of the exercise should briefly describe the process and introduce the purpose of this particular exercise in words such as the following: "The care you provide for another will be enhanced if you are comfortable receiving care. It is harder for most people to receive care than to give it. This exercise will lead you through an experience of receiving care from another person. During the exercise you will become aware of your vulnerability, discern points of resistance to receiving care, and experience the satisfaction of receiving care graciously. There will be several pauses during the exercise to allow for reflection, and time at the end of the exercise for writing your reflections."

Make sure that everyone is supplied with pencils and paper and seated at a table or supplied with pads on which they can write with ease. The writing should flow out of the experience, so it is important to minimize distractions like looking for paper and pencil or not have a good writing surface. Suggest to the participants that key words or phrases are often more useful than full sentences in capturing the flow of the experience. To facilitate the writing, provide participants with the questions found at the end of this exercise on either a photocopied sheet or a chalkboard or newsprint.

Guided Imagery
Read the following slowly, pausing as indicated.

Let yourself relax in the chair that supports your weight, and make yourself as comfortable as you can ... letting your eyes close so you can look inward and avoid outside distractions ... listening only to the sound of my voice as I guide you to a quiet place inside yourself ... letting all other sounds and all other distracting thoughts fade into the background ... allowing yourself to relax into this experience of receiving care ... becoming aware of your breathing in its smooth and natural rhythm ... a rhythm in perfect harmony with the rest of your body ... breathing in the breath of life ... breathing in the Spirit of God, who brings healing into your life ... breathing out fear and anything that keeps you from receiving care from God and others ... breathing in ... breathing out ... receiving ... releasing ... receiving the breath of life, the breath of God ... releasing everything that troubles and distracts you ... sitting in quiet and calm ... aware only of the sound of my voice and the gentle movement of your breathing, breathing that brings peace and quiet and readiness for receiving ... waiting for the movement of the Spirit of God deep within you … aware of seeing with more than your eye, of hearing with more than your ear, of knowing with more than your mind. *(Pause for 30 seconds.)*

Take a few moments in the quiet of this place to reflect back over the past months and years to some of the personal crises you have faced, times when you felt helpless and vulnerable and in need of care from God and others. It may be a physical illness or an accident. It may be the loss of a parent or someone else whom you loved. It may be a loss of faith. It may be something that seems minor now but at the time felt grave and overwhelming.

Imagine yourself floating down the stream of your life and letting memories emerge spontaneously. As you recall personal crises when you were in need of care, open your eyes just enough to jot down a word or two as a reminder of the crisis. Don't analyze or second-guess your intuitions by asking, "Why this crisis?" Though you may not have thought about a particular crisis for years, trust your intuition to identify what is important. I'll give you two minutes of quiet reflection for this journey through time to identify crisis events in your life. *(Pause for 2 minutes.)*

Reflecting on the list of crises you've created, choose one in which you felt most vulnerable and in need of care. *(Pause for 15 seconds.)* Reenter that experience with the aid of your memory and imagination. Where were you at the time the crisis occurred? How did it happen? Recall with your mind and your heart your feelings of vulnerability, your helplessness, your lack of control. *(Pause for 30 seconds.)*

How did you cope with the crisis? Did you feel that you had to handle it alone? If no one offered to help, were you able to ask for the help you needed? Reflect for a moment on any resistance you felt to receiving care. If there was some resistance or resentment on your part, what prompted it—something in you or something in the person providing care? I'll give you a moment to reflect on what it is like for you to be in need of care but hesitant to receive it or ask for it. *(Pause for 1 minute.)*

Is there a crisis of illness or loss that you are faced with in the present? How are you coping with this crisis? Are you handling it alone? If no one has offered to help, are you able to ask for the help you need? Reflect on what it is like to need care but find yourself hesitant to receive it or ask for it. *(Pause for 30 seconds.)*

(Read the questions in the next two paragraphs slowly, pausing briefly after each one.)

If you did receive care in your time of need, did someone offer to help or did you ask for it? Were you uncomfortable in responding to the offer of help or asking for it? What was positive in the experience of receiving care? Did that come as a surprise? Be aware of your weaknesses and strengths in asking for help and responding to offers of help without judging or criticizing your behavior. I'll give you a moment to explore the experience of asking for or responding to offers of help in a time of great need. *(Pause for 1 minute.)*

Did you feel in need of spiritual support in this crisis? Did you ask for or respond to an offer of spiritual care? Were you conscious of God's presence and support? If so, did you pray that God would be present or were you simply aware of that presence in your time of need? What difference did that make? *(Pause for 30 seconds.)*

If not in memory, then in your mind's eye imagine a friend, a nurse, offering to pray with you. *(Pause for 15 seconds.)* What is your reaction? Are you surprised? Gratified? Embarrassed? I'll give you a moment to reflect on what it is like for you to receive spiritual care. *(Pause for 30 seconds.)*

Turning your attention to the present, consider how well prepared you are for meeting whatever crises life may have in store for you and how willing you are to accept help or ask for it in your time of need. After a moment or two of interior reflection, write whatever comes to you when you say to yourself, "If I were seriously ill or facing some other personal crisis, what I would need most from those who are caring of me is…" Then ask yourself, "Aware of my need for help, what would keep me from receiving it or asking for it?" *(Allow 10–15 minutes for writing.)*

Jesus Receiving Care

Introduction

For those who are unfamiliar with guided imagery, the leader of the exercise should briefly describe the process and introduce the purpose of this particular exercise in words such as the following: "We rarely think of Jesus as needing care. The Gospels focus almost exclusively on the adulthood of Jesus and portray him as the master caregiver we are to emulate. In addition, we may mistakenly assume that Jesus had resources to draw on that were not available to mere mortals such as you and me. Yet if we read carefully the portrayal of Jesus in the Gospels, we'll see that he was as much in need of care as any person ever born— perhaps more so, because of his great suffering. Jesus especial- ly needed care as an infant and in his final hours on earth, and he received it graciously. This exercise is designed to enable you to receive care as graciously as Jesus did. There will be several pauses during the exercise to allow for reflection, and time at the end of the exercise for writing your reflections."

Make sure that everyone is supplied with pencils and paper and seated at a table or supplied with pads on which they can write with ease. The writing should flow out of the experience, so it is important to minimize distractions like looking for paper and pencil or not having a stable writing surface. Note that key words or phrases are often more useful than full sentences in capturing the flow of the experience.

Guided Imagery
Read the following slowly, pausing as indicated.

Let your body relax in the place where you are sitting … releas- ing all the tension within your body … feeling tension melt away like snow under the rays of a warm sun ... letting your eyes close or keeping them focused on one particular spot to shut out all distractions ... concentrating your attention on inner aware- ness ... breathing naturally and slowly ... receiving the life-giv- ing oxygen of the air around you and releasing all tensions and distracting thoughts ... breathing in ... and breathing out ... receiving the breath of life ... releasing all worry and tension ... feeling the relaxation deepen ... letting the thoughts that pop into your head simply float away like balloons drifting toward the sky ... breathing a prayer of thanks for all the blessings you have received—the nurture of parents, the steadfast love and faithfulness of God, daily food and shelter.

In your mind's eye imagine Jesus at the beginning of his life, an infant nestled in the arms of his mother—completely depend- ent, vulnerable, as needy as you were when you were born. Imagine Mary tenderly nursing her newborn and the infant Jesus suckling the nourishment that sustains his life. Having fed her child, Mary hands the infant Jesus to you. Experience the good- ness of holding this tiny child as he rests securely in your arms, fully dependent on your safe holding. Though you know Jesus to be divine as well as human, focus your attention for now on the infant you are holding, vulnerable to all that threatens life, depending on the care he receives from you and all those who love him. Gently rock the babe as he relaxes in your arms, gazes at your face, and then gradually closes his eyes and goes to sleep. *(Pause for 30 seconds.)*

With the aid of your deep memory and imagination, reenter the experience of being held by your mother. Feel the goodness of the holding, the security of strong arms enfolding you, the blessing of being completely cared for, the grace of being loved without conditions and without the expectation that you need to do anything in return. Experience the tender care that God intends for every infant, that God intended for the infant Jesus in the arms of Mary. Enter deeply into the experience of receiving the tender care of one who loves you with an abounding and steadfast love. *(Pause for 30 seconds.)*

Now imagine Jesus at the end of his life, hanging on a cross—vulnerable, dying a painful and lonely death. Hear his cry, "My God, my God, why have you forsaken me?" His disciples have abandoned him and only a few women at the foot of the cross are there to support Jesus in his hour of need. I'll give you a moment to enter as fully as you can into his experience of loneliness and deep need. *(Pause for 30 seconds.)*

Picture yourself as a member of the crowd watching the agonizing death of Jesus. What would you want to do to care for Jesus in his time of need? As his life expires, your eyes are drawn to the figure of Mary at the foot of the cross. As Jesus is taken from the cross after the crucifixion, picture Mary cradling the body of Jesus in her arms, as Michelangelo depicts it in the *Pieta,* caring for Jesus at the time of his death as she had at the time of his birth. *(Pause for 30 seconds.)*

With the aid of your imagination, picture yourself at the end stage of a terminal illness. Imagine yourself being very, very sick. Let images of yourself in progressive stages of physical deterioration form in your mind's eye until there is radical loss of weight, a worn and haggard face that appears older than your natural age. Imagine yourself looking into a mirror and being shocked by what you see. The reality of the irreversible process of the disease comes crashing into your awareness. Experience the feelings and thoughts that accompany the realization of a steady movement toward the end stage of your dying. What seems important to you at this point? Would you want to be alone or with others? How would you want to spend your time? *(Pause for 1 minute.)*

Imagine yourself now in a hospice or a room in your home that has been equipped with everything necessary to meet your physical needs in the last days of your life. Furnish the room in any way you wish. Make it large enough to accommodate as many people as you would wish to be present.

Aware that you are living the last days and hours of your life, who would you like to be taking care of you? It can be anyone, living or dead. *(Pause briefly.)* Choose some of the people that you would like to be there. *(Pause briefly.)* What do you need from them more than anything else in these last days of your life? *(Pause briefly.)* Imagine someone holding you the way Mary held Jesus in Michaelangelo's *Pieta.* Who would you want that to be? Imagine that Jesus is in the room. Ask him to help you in any way that seems appropriate to you. *(Pause briefly.)* Let this experience unfold naturally, paying attention to what you need and how Jesus and others care for you. *(Pause briefly.)* How easy is it for you to receive care?

Take a moment to let the experience deepen, and then as you are ready, write down some of the feelings and thoughts that come from within the experience of receiving care in your dying. Let the writing flow spontaneously without analysis or criticism from the rational side of your brain. Words or phrases may capture the experience better than complete sentences. *(Allow 10–15 minutes for writing.)*

Receiving Care within the Household of Faith

Introduction

Are any among you suffering? They should pray. Are any cheerful? They should sing songs of praise. Are any among you sick? They should call for the elders of the church and have them pray over them, anointing them with oil in the name of the Lord. The prayer of faith will save the sick, and the Lord will raise them up; and anyone who has committed sins will be forgiven. Therefore confess your sins to one another, and pray for one another, so that you may be healed. The prayer of the righteous is powerful and effective.

This is James 5:13-16, the classic text for receiving care in the ancient church. Though often cited as an example of the practice of providing care, the passage is directed to those who are suffering and instructs them in asking for help in time of need. They are to call the elders, who provided pastoral care in the early church, and ask for prayer and the anointing of oil. Though used only rarely today, anointing had the status of a healing sacrament in the early church and only hundreds of years later came to be known as last rites, the preparation of the soul for death. Worthy of note also is that the confession and forgiveness of sins is included in the care provided to those who request it. This is a direct outgrowth of the ministry of Jesus, who often linked healing with forgiveness. See Mark 2:1-12:

When he returned to Capernaum after some days, it was reported that he was at home. So many gathered around that there was no longer room for them, not even in front of the door; and he was speaking the word to them. Then some people came, bringing to him a paralyzed man, carried by four of them. And when they could not bring him to Jesus because of the crowd, they removed the roof above him; and after having dug through it, they let down the mat on which the paralytic lay. When Jesus saw their faith, he said to the paralytic, "Son, your sins are forgiven." Now some of the scribes were sitting there, questioning in their hearts, "Why does this fellow speak in this way? It is blasphemy! Who can forgive sins but God alone?" At once Jesus perceived in his spirit that they were discussing these questions among themselves; and he said to them, "Why do you raise such questions in your hearts? Which is easier, to say to the paralytic, 'Your sins are forgiven,' or to say, 'Stand up and take your mat and walk'? But so that you may know that the Son of Man has authority on earth to forgive sins"—he said to the paralytic—"I say to you, stand up, take your mat and go to your home." And he stood up, and immediately took the mat and went out before all of them; so that they were all amazed and glorified God, saying, "We have never seen anything like this!"

The experience of this guided imagery will be enhanced if you share the history of this practice with the individual or group prior to the exercise, the purpose of which is to enable participants to ask for help in time of need from those in the household of faith who are equipped to provide care. The pastor or priest is the first person we think of, but there are others as well, such as parish nurses, hospital chaplains, Stephen Ministers, and modern-day elders. Though such people are trained and make known their willingness to serve, it is hard for many to accept their offers of care, and harder still to ask for their help.

The words of James are included in the guided imagery. If in your judgment those words would be more effective as an introduction to the guided imagery, they could be read at the close of your introduction and before beginning the guided imagery.

Make sure that everyone is supplied with pencils and paper and seated at a table or supplied with pads on which they can write with ease. The writing should flow out of the experience, so it is important to minimize distractions like looking for paper and pencil or not having a stable writing surface. Note that key words or phrases are often more useful that full sentences in capturing the flow of the experience.

Guided Imagery
Read the following slowly, pausing as indicated.

Let all the tension that has collected in your muscles from the stresses and strains of the day drain slowly away as you settle yourself comfortably in the chair where you are sitting. Take several deep breaths. As you inhale, think the word *receiving*, and as you exhale, think *releasing*. The natural rhythm of your breathing is receiving and releasing, as is the natural rhythm of life. Breathing in ... and breathing out ... receiving ... and releasing. Visualize the tension in your muscles as drops of water being released and forming first a trickle and then a stream, slowly flowing down from your shoulders and arms and chest and every portion of your body until it all drains out the bottom of your feet and hands. As the tension flows away from your body, you will become more and more relaxed, more and more in tune with the natural rhythm of your breathing. *(Pause for 30 seconds.)*

Let your mind drift back over the months and years of your life and recall a time when you were ill or in great distress because of some personal crisis. It need not be a catastrophic illness or event, but any occasion that comes to mind that is associated with suffering and the need for help and support from God and others. I'll give you a moment to recall such occasions and choose one to which you are willing to return with the aid of your memory and imagination. Jot down a word or phrase that will help you recall each occasion and then choose from the list the one that evokes the most feeling. *(Pause for 1 minute.)*

In your mind's eye, recall where you were at the time and what was causing you distress. If you were physically ill, what was hardest about the experience? Was it physical pain and suffering? Was it mental anguish because of uncertainty about the nature of the disease or its prognosis? Was it spiritual distress because your spirit was as wounded as your body? If the experience of suffering was occasioned by something other than physical illness, recall with your heart as well as your mind what contributed to your distress and feelings of helplessness. I'll give you time to reenter that experience as fully as you can. Give yourself permission to feel what you were feeling then without fear that the experience will overwhelm you. It may be helpful to jot down words or phrases that capture this experience. *(Pause for 1–2 minutes.)*

From deep within this experience, reflect on your capacity to cope with it. Are you alone, feeling isolated and unable to cope? How willing are you to share your experience of suffering with people that are part of your life—family, friends, pastor and members of your church, neighbors, and colleagues at work? If not, what has kept you from being more open? Has anyone offered to help you? If so, how have you responded? Have you accepted offers of help and support with gratitude or resisted them? Take a moment to reenter that experience and all the feelings associated with accepting or asking for help. *(Pause for 1 minute.)*

Listen to the words of James as he speaks to the household of faith in an early Christian community: *(Read slowly.)* Are any among you suffering? They should pray ... Are any among you sick? They should call for the elders of the church and have them pray over them, anointing them with oil in the name of the Lord. The prayer of faith will save the sick, and the Lord will raise them up; and anyone who has committed sins will be forgiven. So therefore confess your sins to one another, and pray for one another, so that you may be healed. *(Pause for 15 seconds.)*

Are any among you suffering? They should pray. Do you heed this word of God in your suffering and pray for God's help? *(Pause briefly.)* What do you pray for? *(Pause briefly.)* Are you asking for divine intervention, a miracle? Are you asking for spiritual support, for the inner strength to endure your hour of trial? *(Pause for 30 seconds.)*

Are any among you sick? They should call for the elders of the church and have them pray over them, anointing them with oil in the name of the Lord. Do you heed this word of God when you are sick and call your pastor or parish nurse, or anyone from the household of faith to care for you in the name of the Lord? If not, what keeps you from asking for what you need? Do you feel awkward in asking? Are you equally hesitant in calling your doctor? If not, why not?

Confess your sins to one another, and pray for one another, so that you may be healed. Are you aware of a need for spiritual as well as physical healing? Would you feel comfortable in confessing your sins to an elder or another member of the household of faith? If so, could you request that your pastor come to hear your confession? Knowing that Jesus made a close connection between healing and forgiveness, can you at least request a prayer of forgiveness?

I'll give you some time to reflect on how well you heed the counsel of James when you are sick or suffering from any ailment. Then write for a few moments about what keeps you from asking for the spiritual care you need and what you would like to change in your behavior the next time you are sick or suffering from any form of malady. *(Allow 10–15 minutes for reflection and writing.)*

Asking, Searching, Knocking

Introduction

One of the most familiar of Jesus' parables is about going to a friend at midnight asking for three loaves of bread to feed an unexpected guest (Luke 11:5–13). It's a parable about being persistent in asking for help at a time of need, no matter how inconvenient to the person from whom help is requested. We might say, "Couldn't the man have waited until the next morning to ask for bread?" But Jesus wanted to make a point: that we should be as assertive in requesting help as the man banging on the door at midnight and refusing to take no for an answer.

The context of this parable, following Jesus' instruction about prayer and concluding with the assurance that God answers prayer, makes it clear that the friend in the parable to whom the request is made is God. It would be more accurate to say that "the friend," who is not identified, is at least God. God does answer prayer, but God's care is mediated to us through friends and family. Thus to request help from a fellow Christian is to request help from God. To receive care from a fellow Christian is to receive care from God. As Jesus said in the parable of the last judgment, "Just as you did it to one of the least of these who are members of my family, you did it to me" (Matthew 25:40).

If there is sufficient time, include the writing that is suggested in the last paragraph of this exercise, though this activity is optional. Make sure that everyone is supplied with paper and pencils or pens at the beginning of the exercise in order not to interrupt a smooth transition from the guided imagery experience to the reflective writing. This exercise would lend itself well to a brief discussion period at the end of the writing activity. If the writing is included, urge participants to let the writing flow directly out of the experience, avoiding abstract ideas and general principles as much as possible.

Either at the beginning or the end of your introduction of this parable about asking for help, read this portion of the parable:

Suppose one of you has a friend, and you go to him at midnight and say to him, "Friend, lend me three loaves of bread; for a friend of mine has arrived, and I have nothing to set before him." And he answers from within, "Do not bother me; my children are with me in bed; I cannot get up and give you anything." I tell you, even though he will not get up and give him anything because he is his friend, at least because of his persistence he will get up and give him whatever he needs.

So I say to you, Ask, and it will be given you; search, and you will find; knock, and the door will be opened for you. For every one who asks receives, and everyone who searches finds, and for everyone who knocks, the door will be opened.

Guided Imagery
Read the following slowly, pausing as indicated.

Be as relaxed as you can in the chair where you are sitting. Be aware of your breathing as you take several deep breaths, breathing in the breath of life … and breathing out tension and stress … breathing in the breath of life … and breathing out tension and stress … breathing in the breath of life … and breathing out

tension and stress … feeling more and more relaxed each time
you breathe … breathing in the breath of life that comes from
God, and breathing out all the tension and stress that come with
your current distress.

Imagine that you are in a situation of severe distress, faced
with a problem that you cannot resolve without the help of
someone else. It can be any situation that comes to mind, maybe
something that's happened to you or someone else in the past,
maybe some situation that you've always dreaded and hoped
would never happen (like a fall from a bike resulting in a spinal
compression fracture), maybe something from a story you've
read or a movie you've seen—any situation where you know that
you need help. The help you need might be for yourself or for
someone else. I'll give you a moment to imagine such a situation and experience what it would be like. Consider where it is
happening, who else might be involved, and the kind of help you
need. *(Pause for 1 minute.)*

Think about a friend you might go to for help. You know in
advance this is not a good time to make this request, that it
would be inconvenient to your friend, that she or he would have
to give up something important in order to respond to your
request. Would you be willing to ask anyway? If you are hesitant
to do so, ask yourself what is holding you back. Do you feel that
it's too much to ask? Are you willing to allow your friend to
respond to your request, or are you inclined to answer for your
friend and thus not ask at all? What would it take for you to
overcome your resistance and boldly ask for what you need? In
your mind's eye, imagine yourself asking for help and observing
a pained expression on your friend's face. *(Pause for 1 minute.)*

With regret, your friend turns down your request, offering a
valid reason why she or he cannot meet the request. In your
mind's eye, picture the face of your friend as she or he regret-
fully says no to what you ask. *(Pause for 20 seconds.)* What are
you feeling as you hear these words of refusal? How will you

respond? Is your first inclination to accept the reason that has been given and say, "I understand"? Are you likely to feel hurt, perhaps angry, and maybe even bitter? Is your feeling of need strong enough for you to ask again? I'll give you a moment to imagine yourself in that situation and how you would respond. *(Pause for 30 seconds.)* What would it take for you to be persistent and ask again and again, even beg for the help you need? If you find you are unable to do that, ask yourself what's holding you back.

Listen to these words of Jesus: *Ask, and it will be given you; search, and you will find; knock, and the door will be opened for you. For every one who asks receives, and everyone who searches finds, and for everyone who knocks, the door will be opened.* Do you believe those words? Do you trust the promises that accompany Jesus' urging you to ask, to search, to knock? Do you think he was talking only about prayers made directly to him with the expectation that they will be answered directly by him? Or do you think Jesus was suggesting that you ask a friend or a fellow member of your church with full confidence that Jesus answers prayer through those who are his hands and feet? Do you believe that Jesus wants you to be persistent in your asking, your searching, your knocking? I'll give you a moment to reflect on how your behavior would be different if you fully trusted the promises of Jesus in these words: *Ask, and it will be given you; search, and you will find; knock, and the door will be opened for you. For every one who asks receives, and everyone who searches finds, and for everyone who knocks, the door will be opened.* *(Pause for 1 minute.)*

As you are ready, express in writing what it was like to hear the words of Jesus in this parable and his not-so-gentle reminders of the goodness of your asking, searching, and knocking. Reflect on what you've learned in this experience and what, if anything, you'd like to change in your behavior as a result of this experience. *(Allow 10–15 minutes for writing.)*

Receiving Care: The Art of Dying

Introduction

From the 13th to the 15th century, when wars and the plague decimated the population of Europe, the theme of death dominated both art and literature. The genre of literature that reflected this theme was called "The Art of Dying." Unable to escape death, people became preoccupied with the importance of dying well and turned to manuals to learn this art. Paintings from this period depict the dying person in bed, surrounded by a roomful of family members and fellow Christians, along with clergy and sometimes physicians. There was a carefully prescribed ritual for the occasion, which included receiving forgiveness from God and others for past wrongs; last rites to prepare the soul for its departure from the body; and a departing message from the person who is dying.

Until recently the modern era had been characterized by its denial of death and the increasing isolation of the dying in hospitals, surrounded by machines to prolong life, and dying in the cold and sterile environment of a hospital room. Fortunately, that is changing somewhat with the growing hospice movement and a new generation of manuals on the art of dying. Instead of being treated as an object of physical care, as in modern medicine, the dying person is seen as a person whose primary need is spiritual care.

Medical science is concerned with the *what* (cause) of dying, while hospice care is concerned with the *how* (process) of dying. As soon as the focus shifts to how a person dies, receiving care becomes central to the process. But it is best not to wait until you are a candidate for hospice to initiate this process. Why? Because you are likely to die in the same way that you live, including the way you receive care. If you have trouble with good-byes now, you'll have trouble with good-byes then. If you resist care now, you'll resist care then. So now is the time to learn the art of dying, which at its core is the art of receiving care.

There may be some who will feel uncomfortable imagining their own dying. They should of course be given the opportunity to excuse themselves or remain as participant observers. I have made extensive use of guided imagery for dying and grieving , and I have never heard a participant say that it was a bad experience. The opposite is true. Christians are comforted in imagining this experience within the arms of a loving God.

Introduction

To prepare participants for this exercise, provide them with some of the background information contained in the above paragraphs. Explain to them that you will be leading them into a gospel-centered experience of dying. Rather than heightening their anxiety about death, assure them that they will be comforted by this experience and be better prepared to face death without fear whenever it comes.

Guided Imagery

Read the following slowly, pausing as indicated.

Sitting in the quiet and calm of this protected space with eyes closed, removed from the noise and busyness of the outside world, uncross your arms and legs, and find a relaxed position for your body ... becoming aware of your breathing ... breathing in and breathing out ... feeling yourself gradually becoming one with your breathing ... adapting yourself to the natural rhythm of your breathing ... feeling the tensions of the day float away ... letting your body feel more and more relaxed, tensions draining away like water flowing down the side of a hill. In the quiet and calm of your inner space, so relaxed that your body feels as though it is floating in air ... feeling the goodness of being alive ... feeling the wonder of the gift of life ... the gift of breathing ... steadily and quietly. *(Pause for 20 seconds.)*

With the aid of your imagination, picture yourself in the office of your physician. You are there because you have not been feeling well: unexplained tiredness, poor appetite and loss of weight, a persistent cough that won't go away. You've had a series of tests, and you are there to get the results, hoping that all you need is a prescription for something that will make you feel better. Instead you hear your physician informing you that you have an incurable cancer that may or may not respond to treatment that might prolong your life for two to five years. Picture the face of your doctor and pay attention to his or her tone of voice as you hear this news. As you listen to this devastating news, do you feel coldness or caring from your doctor? Will he or she be a source of comfort as well as medical expertise in the coming months? In addition to the support you know you will receive from family and friends, are you likely to turn to your doctor for emotional and spiritual support? I'll give you a moment to let this scene unfold in your mind's eye. *(Pause for 1 minute.)*

Imagine yourself leaving the doctor's office, shaken by the news of your life-threatening illness. Where will you go? With whom, if anyone, do you wish to talk? Let yourself spontaneously choose where you would like to go and whether you feel a need to share this news and, if so, with whom. Maybe you need some time to yourself and would like to go to a church and sit in silence or pray. You may well want to go directly home and talk to loved ones there who are waiting to hear about your doctor's visit. Or perhaps you'd like to go to a good friend or pastor with whom you are comfortable in sharing your deepest feelings. *(Pause for 30 seconds.)*

If you feel a need to keep this news to yourself and talk to no one except perhaps God, ask yourself why you are reluctant to seek out others. Do you want to spare others and shoulder this burden all on your own? Are you hesitant to admit your feelings of vulnerability and helplessness, preferring instead to minimize its seriousness? With whom might you be willing to express your feelings openly?

If and when you choose to share this devastating news with someone, what would you need and want from the person? Is your primary need to have someone just listen with compassion and understanding, without offering advice or protesting anything you say? Are you eager for reassurance that it will all be okay, that the treatment will be effective, that you'll soon feel better? Do you want spiritual support, the assurance that God is and will be with you, and perhaps a prayer for the healing presence of God? Or would you simply like to be held, as an assurance that you are not alone? I'll give you a moment to reflect on your hopes and expectations of care from those you trust. *(Pause for 1 minute.)*

The cancer has been aggressive and is no longer amenable to treatment. You realize that the time of your death is rapidly approaching. Imagine yourself being very, very sick. Let images of yourself in progressive stages of physical deterioration form in your mind's eye until there is radical loss of weight, and a worn and haggard face that appears older than your natural age. Imagine yourself looking into a mirror and being shocked by what you see. Experience the feeling and thoughts that accompany the process of realizing your movement toward the end stages of your dying. What seems important to you at this point? Would you want to be alone or with others? How would you want to spend your time? *(Pause for 90 seconds.)*

Imagine yourself now in a hospice or a room in your home that has been equipped with everything necessary to meet your physical needs in the last days of your life. Furnish the room any way you wish, making it large enough to accommodate as many people as you wish to be present. Aware that you are living the last days and hours of your life, what is it that you need most at this time? *(Pause briefly after each of the following questions.)*

Whom would you like to have caring for you? ... Choose some of the people you would like to be there ... What do you need from them more than anything else in these last days of your life? ... How easy would it be for you to ask for the help you need? ... What would give you the greatest feeling of comfort and assurance? ... Would you want prayers ... or hymns ... or psalms ... or gospel assurances? As you feel ready, let the experience of being cared for in these last days find expression in your writing. *(Allow 15–20 minutes for writing.)*

Meditation

Meditation is a state of alert and spacious calm that is conducive to interior reflection and a deeper-than-intellectual awareness of the abiding and healing presence of God. Meditation is a common practice in most religions, including Christianity. There are many different methods for doing meditation, but interior reflection and inner awareness are common to all.

It may seem strange to you, as it did to me at one time, to think of meditation as receiving care. I have had a daily practice of meditation for many years, but it was not until I was well into this project that I first thought of meditation as receiving care. I was doing nothing different from my usual practice one day, but I was quite unexpectedly suffused with a powerful sense of being cared for.

As I reflected on this experience later, I initially thought of this as self-care, but somehow that did not fit. My sense of self is subdued during meditation. Basic to the practice of meditation is quieting the mind and drawing the self away from preoccupation with its agenda. The more I reflected on the sense of being cared for, the more I realized that my experience in meditation is one of releasing cares and concerns and receiving blessings and peace in return. Above all, meditation is an experience of receiving from God, being cared for by God, within God's embrace, in God's hands. That fit better than the idea that

I was caring for myself or doing anything at all, for that matter.

My perception of meditation as receiving was reinforced by Thomas Keating's method of centering prayer as a contemporary practice for renewing the Christian tradition of contemplative prayer. He describes centering prayer as a restructuring of consciousness that "empowers one to perceive, relate, and respond with increasing sensitivity to the divine presence in, through, and beyond everything that exists."

The method of centering prayer is very simple. Set aside 30 minutes in a quiet place, close your eyes, and choose a sacred word that expresses the intention of opening yourself and surrendering to God. The sacred word can be any word that has a strong association with God's presence; common choices are *come, peace,* or *love.* Centering prayer is a process for receiving God, though Keating rightly notes that "receiving is one of the most difficult kinds of activity there is," even in an exercise that is designed for opening yourself to the presence of God.

Meditation is not for everyone. For many, listening to sacred music is their most profound experience of receiving God. Several years ago I happened to be passing through Carmel, California, on a trip from Big Sur to San Francisco. It was the last day of the annual Bach festival that Carmel hosts each year, and the *B Minor Mass* was to be the final concert. Fifteen minutes before the concert I checked at the box office to see if there was even a remote possibility I might be able to attend. As the attendant was explaining that the concert had been sold out for weeks, someone approached with a ticket he couldn't use.

I regard Bach's *B Minor Mass* as the most profound Christian expression of faith that has ever been set to music. The serendipity of receiving a last-minute ticket to a performance of this magnificent music by superb Bach experts transformed this concert into one of the most profound experiences of receiving God's grace that I have ever known.

What is it that enhances the experience of receiving God in meditation or music? There are many factors that might be cited, but surely one of them is the profound experience of receiving. The goodness of the experience can unfold without you wondering how to respond or whether such a rich experience of receiving is deserved. The ego is relaxed. No need to attend to the presence of another, to actions outside the self, to observe or be observed.

Conclusion

We know, at least theoretically, how dependent we are all the time on the care of others—totally dependent in relation to God and interdependent in all other relationships, though the balance constantly shifts between giving and receiving care. And who among us is not grateful for the care we receive? Gratitude is at the heart of most every Christian's spirituality. The church's ministry will more perfectly reflect the ministry of Jesus if we can lessen some of our negative feelings and attitudes about receiving care and enhance our ability to ask for and receive the care we need.

When I taught courses on death and dying to university students, I told them they needed to be in touch with their own dying before they could be fully present in caring for those who are dying. The same is true for receiving care. If we focus almost exclusively on giving care and ignore our own need for receiving care, it will be reflected in the kind of care we give. The mercy and love we feel will be expressed without a full appreciation of how it is received.

All of us receive care all the time, though rarely do we pay attention to the experience. Children certainly don't reflect on the experience, though they are totally dependent on the care they receive. Care is readily received and given among friends and families without much thought as long as a balance between giving and receiving is maintained. Awareness heightens, however, when we become needy and dependent because of illness or loss. Nobody likes being vulnerable and dependent. Thus heightened awareness of receiving care is almost inevitably associated with negative feelings, at least initially.

It is difficult to reverse negative feelings about receiving care after the onset of a dependence that will not likely end in a short time. The thesis of this book is that receiving care is a practice of faith that comes naturally to children who trust their parents and adults who care for each other in interdependent relationships. Heightened awareness of this experience in normal, healthy relationships will better prepare us for times when the balance is upset and we become heavily dependent on the care of others. In the language of public health, we need to pay more attention to prevention than to cure.

This takes practice. The purpose of practice is to focus attention and improve skill. Receiving care is a skill that can be learned. A sermon on receiving care, a topic in an adult class, personal witness on the part of someone who has received long-term care—all are ways to raise consciousness among congregational members and prepare the way for participation in a workshop. Giving the practice of receiving care the visibility it deserves in the life of a congregation can be a blessing to its members by preparing them to receive care in their time of need. Pastors, parish nurses, and other leaders in wellness ministry should be intentional in inviting people to workshops that help participants develop skills in receiving care.

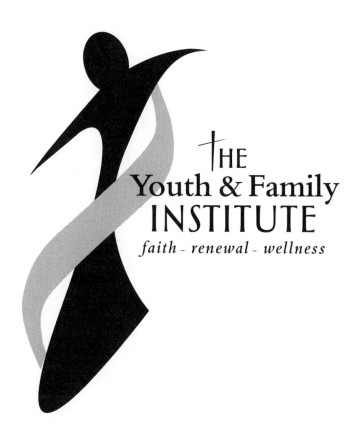

THE
Youth & Family
INSTITUTE
faith ~ renewal ~ wellness

appendix

BIBLIOGRAPHY

SURVEY FORMS

BIBLIOGRAPHY

Dorothy Bass, ed. *Practicing our Faith.* San Francisco: Jossey-Bass, 1997.

Dorothy Bass, *Receiving the Day: Christian Practices for Opening the Gift of Time.* San Francisco: Jossey-Bass Publishers, 2001.

Hector Chevigny, *My Eyes Have a Cold Nose.* New Haven: Yale University Press, 1946.

Thomas Droege, *The Healing Presence: Spiritual Exercises for Healing, Wellness, and Recovery.* Minneapolis: The Youth & Family Institute, 1996. Available at: 1-877-239-2492.

Thomas Keating, *Open Mind, Open Heart.* N.Y.: Continuum, 1986.

Wendy Lustbader, *Counting on Kindness: The Dilemmas of Dependency.* N.Y.: The Free Press, 1991.

Robert F. Murphy, *The Body Silent.* N.Y.: Henry Holt & Co., 1987.

Irving Kenneth Zola, *Missing: A Chronicle of Living with a Disability.* Philadelphia, Temple U. Press, 1982.

For more resources on living well in Christ see
The Youth & Family Institute's catalog on the Web site:
www.youthandfamilyinstitute.org.

SURVEY FORM #1:
SHARING EXPERIENCES IN RECEIVING CARE

Recall a time when it was difficult for you to ask for or receive care. What hindered you?

Recall a time when someone refused the care you offered. How did that make you feel? What did you learn about receiving care?

Recall a time when you needed help but no one offered it. Were you able to ask for what you needed?

Based on your experience, what are the greatest barriers to receiving care? List the things that make it difficult for you to receive care.

What changes in your attitude/behavior would make you a better care receiver?

What attitudes/behaviors do you observe in caregivers that annoy you?

What help do you get from your church in learning to receive care?

Recall a story of someone who is a good model for you on how to receive care graciously.

Is it better to give than to receive? Why?

SURVEY FORM #2:
SHARING EXPERIENCES IN RECEIVING CARE

The gospel is about receiving God's love and forgiveness as pure gift, without any merit or worthiness in us. God cares for us and we receive it gratefully. Are the roles ever reversed? Do you ever think of God as in need of our care?

Do you ever think of Jesus as needy? If so, what stories in the Bible would support this view?

Have you ever heard a sermon on receiving care? Has there been anything in your church experience that has helped you receive care more graciously?

If you were suffering from physical, emotional, or spiritual distress, would you accept an offer of help from a Stephen Minister? Would this be more or less difficult than receiving care from your pastor? What makes one more difficult than the other?

SURVEY FORM #3:
SHARING EXPERIENCES IN RECEIVING CARE

Recall a time in your life when you acted as a caregiver to some-one in physical, emotional, or spiritual distress. Describe how this person received the care you provided. Was your care requested, resisted, or received graciously? As best you can, describe his or her feelings and behavior as a care receiver.

Recall a time in your life when you received care at a time when you were physically, emotionally, or spiritually distressed. Describe your feelings, thoughts, and perceptions of yourself in the role of a care receiver. Did you ask for help? Did you resist it when offered? Were you able to receive it graciously? How did the behavior of the caregiver affect the way you received care?

QUESTIONS ABOUT ATTITUDES AND FEELINGS WHEN RECEIVING CARE

1. What are your feelings about receiving care, both asking for help and responding to an offer of help?

2. What differences are you aware of when the offer of help comes from family, from friends, from members of your congregation, or from your minister?

3. What social conventions and feeling rules are you aware of when you are the recipient of care from family, from friends, from members of your congregation, or from your minister?

4. In which of those relationships are you likely to feel tension between what is expected of you and what you feel? Think of an example. Were you able to resolve the tension? If so, how?

5. What changes would you like to make, if any, in your feelings and attitudes about receiving care?

QUESTIONS ABOUT SELF-UNDERSTANDING AND SELF-CONCEPT IN RECEIVING CARE

1. How would you describe yourself (feelings and attitudes) when in a situation where it is appropriate either to ask for help or to respond to an offer of help?

2. How might that differ in relationship to family, friends, congregational members, and pastor/priest?

3. What in your past experience has shaped those feelings and attitudes? For example, how are you different from your parents, your siblings, your friends?

4. What changes would you like to make, if any, in your attitude about receiving care?

THE
Youth & Family
INSTITUTE
faith - renewal - wellness